# values sell

## TRANSFORMING PURPOSE INTO PROFIT THROUGH CREATIVE SALES AND DISTRIBUTION STRATEGIES

By
### Nadine A. Thompson
### Angela E. Soper

D1615973

**16**
EasyRead Large

# Copyright Page from the Original Book

## Values Sell

Berrett-Koehler Publishers, Inc.
235 Montgomery Street, Suite 650
San Francisco, California 94104-2916
Tel: (415) 288-0260, Fax: (415) 362-2512
www.bkconnection.com

Ordering information for print editions
*Quantity sales.* Special discounts are available on quantity purchases by corporations, associations, and others. For details, contact the "Special Sales Department" at the Berrett-Koehler address above.
*Individual sales.* Berrett-Koehler publications are available through most bookstores. They can also be ordered directly from Berrett-Koehler: Tel: (800) 929-2929; Fax: (802) 864-7626; www.bkconnection.com
*Orders for college textbook/course adoption use.* Please contact Berrett-Koehler: Tel: (800) 929-2929; Fax: (802) 864-7626.
*Orders by U.S. trade bookstores and wholesalers.* Please contact Ingram Publisher Services, Tel: (800) 509-4887; Fax: (800) 838-1149; E-mail: customer.service@ingrampublisherservices.com; or visit www.ingram publisherservices.com/Ordering for details about electronic ordering.

Berrett-Koehler and the BK logo are registered trademarks of Berrett-Koehler Publishers, Inc.

Cataloging-in-Publication Data are available from the Library of Congress.

First Edition
Paperback print edition ISBN 978-1-57675-421-4
PDF e-book ISBN 978-1-57675-520-4

2007-1

Cover design: Leslie Waltzer, Crowfoot Design

Interior design and production: Beverly Butterfield, Girl of the West Productions

Editing: PeopleSpeak

# TABLE OF CONTENTS

*For all the women and men who have an idea
and pursue it with passion—and who have
the courage to keep going with bold determination
when told their idea will never work*

# Letter from the Editor of the Social Venture Network Series

Every year more than one million new businesses form in the United States. Most of them fail within a few years. Conventional wisdom has it that the principal reason for such widespread failure is a lack of capital, but after reading *Values Sell,* I'm not so sure.

Consider the advice you're likely to get from the average business consultant, banker, accountant, or business school professor: "Keep your costs low, keep your eye on the cash, and keep your customers happy." You may walk away with the tragically misguided impression that building a successful business is a lot like baking a cake, simply combining a teaspoon of this, a pinch of that, and a dash of something else—all readily available ingredients, easy to find on the shelf.

Anyone with any practical business experience knows that's bunk. As Nadine Thompson and Angela Soper make abundantly clear in this inspired little volume, a successful small business requires a whole lot more than a competitive product or service, tight cash management, and good customer relations—or any combination of readily identifiable ingredients.

In fact, as you'll learn in the following pages, success in business depends far more on intangible factors such as vision, commitment, and passion than on any of the more familiar building blocks of commerce. By focusing tightly on the critical question of sales and distribution, Thompson and Soper show how clarity of vision, consistency of values, a collaborative spirit, a passion to teach all who will listen, enduring strategic alliances, and a willingness to empower those around you will compensate for shortages of some of the more traditional ingredients.

*Values Sell* is jam-packed with colorful and inspiring vignettes from some of America's most enterprising small companies. In these pages, your eyes will be opened and your spirits lifted through the experiences of dynamic enterprises such as Birkenstock USA, Tweezerman, Mountain Equipment Co-op, French Meadow Bakery & Cafe, Tom's of Maine, Earthbound Farm, and Putumayo World Music.

Each of these and the approximately two dozen other outstanding small companies profiled in *Values Sell* has prospered by building sales and distribution strategies that embody the uniqueness of its vision and the depth of its values. Thompson and Soper will help you understand how the roots of your own approach to sales and distribution can be found within the values you bring to your work and not in any formula or any textbook. If you're running a small or midsized business, or just thinking about starting one, you'll close the covers of this book with a far deeper appreciation of some of the biggest challenges of business today and how you can surmount them.

And one more thing: you'll enjoy reading this delightful little book, and I predict you'll want to pass it along to a friend. It's that good.

Mal Warwick
Berkeley, California
February 2007

# Preface

Songwriters and romance novelists may say it is love that makes the world go round, but we venture to say it is innovation. When it comes to selling products and getting them from the manufacturer to the end customer, creativity can mean the difference between lackluster (or no) sales that leave products languishing in the warehouse and products that fly off the shelves and keep freight trucks rolling on the highway.

For businesses just starting out, money may be tight. You may not be able to afford splashy advertising campaigns or an expensive public relations firm that can help you obtain valuable media exposure. But you can find creative ways to draw attention to your product and business. You can seek out strategic alliances with like-minded businesses or organizations that will help you promote, sell, or distribute your product without huge costs. And you can use your values to move your business forward.

This is the purpose of *Values Sell: Transforming Purpose into Profit Through Creative Sales and Distribution Strategies.* Our goal is to share ideas and techniques that have proved successful for other small businesses and to provide you with strategies that will help you develop your own "creative game plan" for increasing sales and more efficiently distributing your product.

Adding the words "values-driven" or "socially responsible" to a business's goals adds a new paradigm to the success equation. Not only must you, as an entrepreneur, take pains to ensure growth for your business, you must make sure your socially responsible mission marches proudly alongside each step of your business's development. If you're just starting out on such a journey, the road can be confusing and fraught with obstacles that threaten to derail you, whether from a profit standpoint or from a values standpoint.

In this book we will focus on ways to foster and manage sales and distribution techniques that will keep your socially responsible business moving forward. You will meet a number of business owners and true entrepreneurs who have grappled with the conundrum of increasing profits as they retain their individual, socially responsible agendas. We have gleaned "words of sales wisdom" from a wide spectrum of people in the marketplace to help you understand that a values-driven business can exist just about anywhere and in any fashion—from the broadcasting of television programs that present issues with a global perspective to innovative, all-natural baked goods that not only turn a profit but also help homeless families get back on their feet.

You'll read inspiring stories about entrepreneurs, some who were prodded into their businesses by redwood splinters, Alabama clay, thirst, and too many bags of salad greens. You'll discover what works—and what doesn't work. And you'll learn that new ideas, flexibility, and a willingness to partner with likeminded individuals often go hand in hand when it comes to meeting goals and increasing sales or broadening the distribution of products.

You'll also discover that "sales and distribution" can cast a wide net in enhancing a business. For the myopic, sales means an exchange of money for goods. For the wise values-driven entrepreneur, sales means a holistic approach to selling your company's mission, your business's merchandise or service, the people behind the business, and your social mission. And it isn't unusual for a sales promotion to have significant positive ramifications in many other areas of the business. For example, a product promotion that helps educate consumers about an environmental issue can result in a number of benefits: greater visibility of your business among the public at large, which means added customers in the long term, more-loyal customers, greater pride among your employees, and of course, increased awareness about the issue you're publicizing.

If you've made a decision to operate a values-driven business that has a specific socially responsible mission, chances are your passion to make a difference is already fueling your drive to sell your products. What you may be lacking is the wherewithal to mesh this passion with effective and creative ways to increase your sales so you can be profitable—and continue to build the business of your dreams.

We will show you how using your values and socially responsible mission as the foundation for your sales efforts—and throwing in some innovation as well—and carefully choosing the way you move your product from manufacturer to end customer can actually enhance your bottom line. Some in the sales world might think the only way to increase sales is to keep all costs as low as possible to maximize profit. This might mean minimizing employee benefits, trimming customer service, or skimping on packaging. The examples we cite in this book will demonstrate that when companies put extra care into how they treat people (from employees and vendors to customers) and how they produce and distribute their prod-ucts—even if it means spending more up front—the results can be highly beneficial.

There's no denying that businesses can be highly successful and provide benefits to the community (added jobs, a boost to overall economic develop-ment, frequent charitable contributions) and never fall under the umbrella of "values-driven businesses." Such companies can generate huge sales, and they may have a distribution infrastructure in place that runs as smooth as silk 24/7. We all know businesses like these, and we most often respect and patronize them frequently. However, a values-driven business creates long-term advantages that can be highly beneficial as the company moves from quarter to quarter in building both sales and a name for itself in the marketplace.

To help you glean the most value from the book's contents, at the beginning of each chapter we've highlighted a specific example—a "Creative Challenge"—shared with us by one of the socially responsible business leaders we interviewed. This example demonstrates the type of lesson that the chapter offers. At the end of each chapter we've boiled down the featured case studies into "Collective Wisdom" you can use in plotting your own sales and distribution strategies. We believe wisdom is obtained through experience—in life, in relationships, most certainly in business. By sharing the situations these businesses have experienced, we hope to help you find ways to increase your profits.

Creating a successful business is far from formulaic. If only entrepreneurs could pick up a manual and follow a diagram to reach the goal of huge profits and a loyal customer base. But everyone knows that such a diagram doesn't exist. However, in a book of this type, an analogy can be a great tool for putting an idea—such as building a business—into perspective.

As we learned how experienced businesspeople built their ventures, we noticed the similarities to making a journey across the sea in a sailboat. First of all, a sailor must have a destination in mind and chart a safe course—leaving the harbor without a navigation plan could be deadly. Such a journey also requires researching what the weather will be like during the trip, what kinds of supplies will be needed, and which equipment will stand up to the task at hand, as well as preparing for emergencies. A properly trained crew is also vital. And a good captain wants a crew that works as a team—if disaster strikes, people must pitch in and work together to avert the crisis.

Sudden changes are not uncommon on the high seas, nor are they uncommon in the business world. Winds can shift abruptly and storms can blow up in a heartbeat, just as sales can suddenly drop off or an important shipment can be delayed or lost. A leader—whether on a sailboat or at the helm of a new business venture—must be prepared to redesign strategies when necessary.

Of course, making an ocean voyage is not all danger and unexpected challenges. Sailors experience moments of jubilation as their boat sails swiftly across the water, with the sails perfectly aligned to capture every knot of wind speed and the sun shining brightly overhead. As an entrepreneur, you will have such moments of exhilaration yourself, and it is important to celebrate your successes and recognize those who have helped you achieve them, just as a good captain toasts his crew upon safely reaching port.

The important point to remember is that building a business successfully means maintaining a vision and supporting it with a plan of action that is often original and bold. However, you must be open to making changes if a challenge—or opportunity—emerges that requires rethinking some aspect of your operation.

We hope the comments from those who agreed to share their knowledge, mistakes, and successes will inspire you to join the growing network of companies that proudly practice social responsibility daily and are finding that remaining true to such values is increasing their sales and overall profitability.

We have written this book with a desire both to gain insight ourselves and to share this information with you, the reader. If you come away with even one idea that helps increase your sales or streamline your distribution system as you make the world a better place, we will feel gratified.

As authors, our job in creating this book was to teach and help people become more successful as values-driven entrepreneurs. An unexpected benefit has been an enhanced awareness about how we look at other companies—and the relationships we form with them.

In effect, this exercise has raised our own standards as consumers.

We realized that whether consciously or subconsciously, we tend to gravitate toward companies that operate with a socially responsible mission or companies whose values we share or admire. Sometimes the matter is as simple as the way a company positions its product in the marketplace. For example, if a company is promoting the beauty of diversity in the world, especially the diversity that exists among women, that kind of campaign resonates with us and makes us more likely to purchase the company's product.

We hope this book will raise your own bar of socially responsible awareness—as both a businessperson and as a consumer. We feel the two perspectives go hand in hand and will help all of us enjoy a more sustainable planet.

# Acknowledgments

## From Nadine's heart

Let me begin by saying that this book would not have been possible without the talent, skill, courage, and patience of my coauthor, Angela Soper. She really deserves 100 percent of the credit for bearing the responsibility of the task. She made a job that at many times felt overwhelming feel doable. Thank you, Angela. You are the best.

Second, I would like to thank the community of Social Venture Network; it is in that community that I have grown as a socially responsible businessperson and learned what it means to walk the talk in this very important facet of doing business. Thanks to Deb Nelson for her friendship and support, for her nominating me to be one of the writers in this series, and most of all for her confidence in me. I owe a huge debt of gratitude to Josh Mailman, and to Melissa Bradley, thank you for just being you. I deeply admire you and all that you do.

Thank you to all of the businesspeople who so willingly and freely gave of their time to do the interviews for the book. You added the richness and depth that we needed to illustrate the fact that *values sell.*

I'm indebted to my business partner, Daniel Wolf, for his generosity and for serving as a living example of doing well by doing good. Daniel, your partnership and generosity has made all of this possible. As someone once said at an SVN meeting, you're not an angel investor but an archangel. You rock, dude!

To the 25,000 consultants who currently make up the Warm Spirit community, thank you for trusting me, following my lead, and sharing your compelling visions with me and the rest of the world. Your fortitude keeps me going.

To Bob (my beloved), thank you for being my love, spiritual mentor, and my rock. You are the deepest blessing in my life. You are a giant with the sweetest, sweetest spirit. Camilla and Isaiah, this is all for the both of you. My love for you motivates me to do better and inspires me to leave the world a better place than when I met it. Camilla and Isaiah, you both are a manifestation of God's love for me; thank you for being patient while I continue to live out my calling and my desire to serve.

Thank you to the entire team at Berrett-Koehler who supported Angela and me, gave us feedback, edited, tossed and turned, and most importantly, welcomed us into your community. I am deeply honored.

# From Angela's heart

It's been said that writing a book of this nature is a team effort. That's a truth we embrace wholeheartedly. And that's why most books include an acknowledgments page like this—so those of us given the task of compiling all of the research and thoughts into one cohesive volume can thank those who made it all possible.

I am grateful to the support offered by Deb Nelson, executive director of Social Venture Network, who answered frantic questions, provided valuable contact information, and is just one heck of a nice person. My sincere appreciation goes to Nadine Thompson for asking me to help with this project and for giving me the chance to get to know so many incredible individuals. Nadine's vision has improved lives all over the country, and she has touched mine in many profound ways as well.

They say a writer is only as good as her or his editor, and I offer heartfelt hugs to Berrett-Koehler Editorial Director Johanna Vondeling, who provided critical direction and support throughout the writing process. I am also indebted to Senior Managing Editor Jeevan Sivasubramaniam, whose sense of humor kept me laughing when challenges erupted. And I can even pronounce his last name now.

Huge thanks go to Rebecca Carter, who expertly and quickly transcribed the many hours of interviews. Not only is she one of the best transcribers on the planet, she has terrific ideas about creating a socially responsible business and offered wonderful insight into how to present some of the comments we recorded. Thanks to my son, Ryan Soper, who was there with a hug and a vote of confidence in a moment of writer's angst and who always, always makes me look beyond the immediate situation.

And finally, applause and kudos and hugs and kisses and everything else to the many company leaders who shared their expertise, their thoughts, and their passion for making a difference in the world with the businesses they operate. They taught us, they inspired us, and they showed us that "doing well by doing good" isn't just a nice phrase—it can be a great way to sell and distribute products successfully.

Nadine Thompson
Exeter, New Hampshire

Angela Soper
Salt Lake City, Utah

February 2007

# Establishing a clear and profitable vision

## THE CREATIVE CHALLENGE: Using your vision to solve problems and develop new strategies for increasing sales

Seventh Generation, maker of nontoxic and environmentally safe household products, was faced with a dilemma regarding its values versus its sales when a large grocery chain that carried the company's products experienced a labor strike. As a company that strives to be a positive force in society, Seventh Generation had to decide whether to sell to the grocer since the strike involved health benefits. The company chose to continue to do business with the grocery chain during the strike but to donate all profits from those sales to the workers' strike fund. This action helped Seventh Generation maintain a good relationship with the grocer's employees, its customers, and the grocer itself, all of which contributed to future sales.

Vision. It's a simple word with huge connotations in the business world. Surely for anyone who has awakened in the middle of the night with a new business idea glowing like a 100-watt bulb in her head, the vision is sparkling clear, illuminating every fiber in her body. Most of us have had such "visionary" moments in our lives. Maybe it wasn't a new business idea but a new way to solve a problem or enhance your life or someone else's: an abrupt awareness of that nagging reason you couldn't balance the checkbook, a sudden insight into why your teenager has been giving you nasty glares for three days, the perfect way to celebrate your parents' wedding anniversary.

There's no discounting such moments of blinding insight when it comes to proposing a new idea. And of course, there's also plenty of room for those who start with a kernel of an idea, work laboriously and painstakingly to nurture it, and allow it to germinate fully before putting it into action. However it is reached and ultimately presented, a vision can be a critical component of creating sales and distribution strategies that move a business forward. In fact, it is often the foundation for many other aspects of a business that can play a role in promoting healthy sales and distribution: marketing, customer service, personnel issues, community outreach, public relations.

In a values-driven business, or socially responsible business, the vision is the torchbearer that leads his or her team proudly over the challenging terrain of business ups and downs. Occasionally this vision may alter its route, adjust for changes in the environment or climate, or even reconfigure the long-term strategy, but it will always maintain a steady course toward the goal at hand. Vision is looking to the horizon and imagining what could be. Vision is daring to head toward that horizon with a true sense of purpose and a plan of action.

In this chapter we will give you examples of business leaders who have established clear and profitable visions as they formulated their companies and then used their visions as strategic allies in selling their products or services. These visions encompassed a socially responsible agenda but were also modeled on sound business principles that took into account a very basic rule of success: people must want what you are selling, the product or service must be of high quality, and consumers must want to purchase it again and again.

Whatever business you're in—or hoping to create—you will be selling. In addition to your product, you will sell your concept to potential investors, you will sell your socially responsible mission, you will sell your brand and what it stands for, and you will sell what you stand for as an individual.

Although this book is about creative sales and distribution strategies, you won't be able to sell effectively unless your business is grounded in a powerful vision. A clear vision will drive you forward and enable you to scale new heights. It can get you through the tough times (and all businesses have them!) and help you adjust when change is required. Lack of vision will stifle you or send you in confusing directions. And if you don't know where you're headed, your investors, your suppliers, your community, and certainly your customers will be confused and may lose confidence in your business and your product. As Angela's writer and attorney friend Danny Quintana says, "It's easy to get where you're going if you know where you're going."[1] Your vision can be that shining, guiding star.

By establishing your vision and the actions that will support it, you will be better able to design and support strong sales and distribution strategies. First, let's take a look at a few socially responsible companies and the particular vision and actual business of each.

Seventh Generation makes nontoxic and environmentally safe household products. It wants to market products that save natural resources, keep toxic chemicals out of the environment, and make the world a safer place—for generations to come. The *vision* is to make the world a safer, healthier place and foster social and environmental change. The *business* is household products.

New Leaf Paper sells recycled paper. The *vision* is to inspire a fundamental shift toward environmental responsibility in the paper industry. The *business* is selling high-quality paper made from recycled content that can replace traditional "new" paper.

Hot Lips Pizza wants to be a positive influence in the community. The *vision* is to find new, sustainable ways of doing business as the company supports local growers. The *business* is selling pizza and homemade soda.

Tom's of Maine, the market leader in health and specialty products, has maintained a *vision* to do what is right for its customers, employees, communities, and environment. The *business* is creating and selling safe, effective products sourced in nature.

If you're just starting down the road of creating a values-driven business, you may occasionally run into challenges as you attempt to manage the social responsibility aspect of your venture with good business practices that boost sales. You may some-times find it tough to keep your values aligned with day-today operations, especially if you're trying to change how people view your product or industry and possibly change *their* way of doing business.

Here we offer some Vision Strategies to help align your vision with sound business principles that will keep you headed toward increased sales.

# VISION STRATEGY NUMBER ONE: Think about how your vision and product combined can improve your customers' business or personal lives.

Keeping a compelling story and a compelling vision in the forefront of your sales efforts can play an important role in moving your business forward. You can use this strategy to relay the message about why your product is worth purchasing and help motivate your sales force.

As you are presenting your product (or service) to customers, it's important that your message be easy to understand. If you clutter your sales pitch with a complex explanation that weaves the details of your socially responsible mission with the benefits of your product, you may confuse the buyer to the point that it's just too much trouble for him to invest in what you're selling.

Another critical component of selling is listening. If you don't know your customer and what he needs or wants, your presentation may fall on deaf ears. Understand what you are selling and to whom you are selling it. Does your presentation need to be tailored for each customer? In other words, is Customer A likely to be more interested in the socially responsible benefits your product or business offers, and is Customer B going to be more interested in the actual product benefits? Consider how you can streamline your message so it is to the point and clear to those listening.

Here are some pointers from Jeff Mendelsohn, founder of New Leaf Paper.

## Making It Compelling

Founded in 1998, New Leaf Paper of San Francisco, California, has grown rapidly the past few years and now does close to $20 million in annual sales. Similar companies were created in the early nineties but have since closed their doors or now operate as small regional companies. So why did New Leaf succeed when the others did not? "I think what we did well was to break into a high commodity business with a proposition that didn't scare people away," says Jeff. "We were able to address their business needs."[2]

One way Jeff and his staff have done this is by putting themselves in the shoes of their customers. "Take off your save-the-world hat," Jeff continues, "and put on the hat of whoever you're selling to, and think about what is going to be compelling to them." Of course, New Leaf has an environmental agenda, but approaching prospective customers with only this part of the mission would not make good business sense, according to Jeff. "People have a hard time selling on more than one platform. They get caught up in the environment and then that's all they'll talk about ... we've always combined the environment with good business ... they come out in the same breath. That's probably one of the reasons why we've been able to be successful."[3]

Key to New Leaf's selling approach is keeping the combined environmental and business message extremely clean and simple. In addition, Jeff stresses the importance of taking a partnership approach to business and emphasizing win-win deals with customers. "Listen to them very carefully," he says, "because, especially at the outset, your preconceived notions about what is going to sell and what is exciting to your customers will be partly right and partly wrong."[4] By listening to your customers, you make them feel appreciated. They also have a chance to be part of your mission if you embrace them in what you're doing.

Combining the company's vision with good business practices and finding a compelling story for each customer enables New Leaf Paper to lead the industry in the development and distribution of environmentally superior printing and office papers.[5] Clearly, New Leaf Paper has found tremendous benefit in adding "compelling" to its business plan as it keeps its values-driven mission and product sales goals aligned.

# VISION STRATEGY NUMBER TWO: Align your vision with your community's interests.

If your business is small, the community in which you operate is probably very important to you. It may be the source of your employees, your customers, and even your suppliers. Therefore, your actions as a businessperson must be in tune with the needs and interests of your community because it includes the people who are supporting you. This strategy can be critical if you face a business challenge or want to sell a product or offer a service that is unfamiliar to your customers. In other words, the more trust and loyalty you develop among those in your community, the better chance you have of maintaining sales, keeping supplies on hand, and meeting shipping deadlines when challenges erupt. Developing strong relationships with those in your community is also important. Listen to their ideas and keep an open dialogue going so you can prevent small issues from turning into large problems.

"Community" is the key word in the next example. And it became key when the entrepreneurs took stock of their business and how they could build a company that matched their personal interest of supporting their community—something they determined was important to them as they were taking over the reins of the family operation and were preparing to "restart" the business.

The players in this story encompass the entire community, which is exactly what the business owners want. The story includes local farmers who wanted to find a new market for a specific product, as well as other local growers who supply the business with organic fruits, vegetables, cheeses, and meats. It also involves vision and putting business practices into place *today* so the business will be one step ahead of larger, more established competitors tomorrow. Remember that your secret weapon for gaining sales in your community may be ingenuity since you probably won't have the advertising dollars or brand awareness of bigger competitors (such as national chains).

Keeping the community's interests in mind helped these entrepreneurs rebuild the business. Their actions help maintain customer loyalty and help the company reduce costs (which helps boost profits) by using local, fresh ingredients that don't have to be imported. Fresh ingredients also make a higher-quality product, which again can help retain and increase sales.

## Serve Your Business by Serving Your Community

Hot Lips Pizza owners David Yudkin and his wife, Jeana Edelman, took over her family's struggling Portland, Oregon, business, which began as a gourmet pizza company in 1984. The enterprise lacked an infrastructure, and it grew too fast. David and Jeana managed to pay off the sizable debt that had accrued and then took stock of the business and asked themselves why they were doing it and what they wanted from it.

One of the priorities for the couple was to be a positive influence on their community. About that time, David attended a presentation by Natural Step (an international organization created to accelerate global sustainability) and was influenced by Natural Step's advocacy of businesses' having a role in addressing the environmental issues of the time.

David also wanted to create a better place for his children, just as his parents and immigrant grandparents had done for him. And finally, he knew supporting his community, specifically by purchasing his ingredients from local farmers, was parallel with having a quality product. From all of this, David determined that the business's competitive edge was innovation, and innovation has been key to everything David has been doing since. His out-of-the-box thinking has garnered Hot Lips publicity on HBO and in the *Wall Street Journal, Forbes* magazine, and other publications, and it resulted in the small pizza chain receiving Portland's Businesses for an Environmentally Sustainable Tomorrow BEST Business Award in 2002.[6]

As David was recreating his business, a billboard promoting a major pizza chain's use of sun-dried tomatoes made him realize he had to find a creative way to offer his customers a great product. He believes an innovative approach to doing business and building sales has to be tied to real issues that are part of the community.

To help the company put its new business model into place, David adopted Natural Step's concept of looking upstream—envisioning where you'd want to be if the world were sustainable. It's called "backcasting," according to David, and it helped him get a vision of his ultimate goals for Hot Lips and understand the steps he had to take to align his company with the future.

Serving the community by buying from the community is important to David and Jeana. Most of the ingredients for their pizzas and locally bottled soda are supplied by local farmers, and many are certified organic. "That's a goal of everything we do," says David.[7] In other words, his ingredients and supplies come from local businesses, so his purchases provide direct benefit to the community.

David is also big on finding solutions to local problems. An example is the way he helped local soft wheat farmers find a market for their wheat, which is used in bread products like his pizza. Because the northwestern area grows and mills mostly hard wheat, the soft wheat farmers had to create a new infrastructure for producing their product. According to David, the time and expense involved in recreating an infrastructure like this is one reason organic and local foods are more expensive.[8]

David used his vision of being a positive influence in his community to solve both a commodity problem and a distribution problem faced by local suppliers. His efforts also gave him a new source for an ingredient he needed to make a quality product and continue to foster goodwill within the community. Actions like this help Hot Lips build a more loyal customer base and greater sales.

## VISION STRATEGY NUMBER THREE: Be open to adjusting your vision as your business grows.

As your company grows, you need to review your objectives and listen to the marketplace, your customers, your suppliers, your employees, and your community to realign your values in a holistic, beneficial manner. For many businesses, this means forming deep relationships with everyone connected to the business and working together to make something larger and more important happen.

When it comes to sales, what you're selling and where it came from is only half the equation. You must also consider how your products are sold and to whom they are sold. When faced with a challenge regarding your sales efforts, creative thinking may go a long way in making the most of a difficult situation. Consider how you can create a win-win-win situation so you, your distributor, and your customers each have a positive outcome.

When Seventh Generation faced the challenge with the grocery chain that we highlighted at the start of this chapter, it was able to engineer a solution that benefited everyone. Although the company gave its profits to the workers on strike and therefore didn't make money on those sales, the goodwill and integrity the company created went a long way toward establishing Seventh Generation as a good company to do business with. Its actions demonstrate how the company makes its values—which go hand in hand with its vision—an essential part of its entire chain of relationships. Its relationship with the retailer continued, customers were still able to buy the company's products, and Seventh Generation was able to show solidarity with the workers on an important issue.[9]

Remember also that your product's value involves more than just its price. If your product resonates with customers on a level that goes beyond a simple exchange of money for an item that serves a purpose, you build brand loyalty that can translate into sales even when a competitor offers a better price.

Next we present more about how Seventh Generation has allowed its vision to evolve to the benefit of growing sales.

# *Evolution of Your Vision Builds Profits*

Jeff Hollender, founder and CEO of Vermont-based Seventh Generation, believes a company's vision evolves over time. But before you can have a vision, you must know who you are and determine your own essence. From the beginning, Jeff focused on offering people avenues that helped them express their idealism, passion, and commitment to a cause larger than themselves and larger than the company. His definition of "people" included managers and employees as well as Seventh Generation's customers, suppliers, partners, and anyone else involved in the company's value and supply chain. "We've tried to be, in the largest sense, a satisfying company to work for and do business with, and a major part of that effort is having a well-developed vision of what it means to be a responsible business and a good corporate citizen," says Jeff.[10]

When Seventh Generation began in 1988, its product tagline was "Products for a Healthy Planet." But over time, company officials saw a larger interest in health and wellness. In 2000, the wellness trend started to propel the natural food industry and began to have a very positive impact on Seventh Generation's sales.

Jeff is a firm believer in the idea that when people purchase a product, more than price comes into play. "At the end of the day," he says, "the question is, What is the perceived value of what you buy?" To him, value is a combination of price, product quality, and other benefits someone receives when purchasing a product, which may play a role in encouraging people to support a company that has values similar to theirs.[11]

A product with a tangible benefit could be one that has a direct impact on a person's health—such as a laundry detergent that makes the rash on a child's face disappear. Such a benefit, Jeff points out, is a powerful motivator when it comes to making a purchasing decision. Jeff believes that the health benefits his products offer have become an important driver for the company, even more so than the environmental benefits and the value of being a responsible business.

In addition to focusing on health and wellness issues and how the company's products impact the customers' lives, Jeff feels the idea of sustainability has expanded. "As you say 'sustainability,' you're no longer talking just about the environment, but you're talking about issues of equity and issues of justice because you can't have sustainability without equity and justice," he adds. This notion has made Seventh Generation increase its focus on the role that business needs to play in the world.[12]

With over eighteen years of experience, Seventh Generation has been "around the block" when it comes to creating a formula for sales success while remaining true to its values-driven mission. As one who started his company as a private venture, took it public, and then turned it back into a private company, Jeff also has a firm grasp on the importance of seeking investors who embrace his vision. Because he has chosen investors who share Seventh Generation's values (coupled with the financial success of the company), he's had no trouble obtaining additional investments from current shareholders.

By expanding its vision in these ways—moving from a primary focus on the environment to a focus on health, broadening the definition of "sustainability," increasing its focus on the role it needs to play in the world, and ensuring that its vision is aligned with its investors'—Seventh Generation has experienced 30 to 40 percent growth every year since about 2000, reports Jeff.[13] That is a very significant way to demonstrate the importance of allowing your vision to evolve over time.

*** 

For companies that have been in business for some time and perhaps have not always had a socially responsible agenda, incorporating values into the business and sales model may offer a unique set of challenges. Unlike a new business that can use its values-driven policies to set sales and distribution strategies right from the start, an established business must find innovative ways to demonstrate its new message and more responsible way of selling products.

Successful companies can and indeed do change how they operate when they adopt a more values-driven focus. We sincerely hope that as issues pertaining to the welfare of our planet and its inhabitants begin to resonate around the world, more and more companies will take steps to make some aspect of the term "socially responsible" part of their mission statement.

But you can't expect changes to occur overnight. You may add new customers, new suppliers, and new distributors as you go about transforming your business into a more socially responsible venture that you believe will boost sales or expand the business in new directions. However, you will likely retain your current customers, suppliers, and distributors as well (not to mention current employees). That means finding novel ways to work with all the people connected to your business so they understand what you're doing and *why* you're doing it. Change is good; change can be refreshing and provide a jolt of new energy. However, change without education can be disruptive.

Once again, it is important to look for the win-win (and beyond) situation your changes can make. Communication is key and involves not only explaining what you're doing but *listening* to those who are affected by your changes. If you take the time to listen and learn, you may discover new ideas that mesh perfectly and profitably with the changes you want to make.

Developing strategic alliances with suppliers or distributors so you can make this new journey with shared
values is also important. You don't have to be a rebel
going it alone; your business likely touches many
people, and the more alliances you can create, the
easier your journey will be. If you can make others
proud to be part of your mission, the transformation
you're after can be a positive experience that sends
ripples far beyond your own business. And isn't that
one element of being a socially responsible organization?

Also remember that if you are committed to changing
how you're doing business, you must walk the talk.
If developing a more environmentally conscious
product is one of your goals, then consider how you
can make a cultural shift in your own operation. Does
this mean creating a recycling program? Using soy-
based inks and recycled paper in your corporate pro-
motional materials? Using nontoxic cleaning products?
Encouraging the use of public transportation among
your employees? Again, your vision, your mission,
and your values must go hand in hand as you set
forth on your transformation and work to create new
and bigger sales.

# VISION STRATEGY NUMBER FOUR:
# Align every aspect of your business

# with your core values to help drive sales.

Think of your values as the fuel that is powering your vehicle as you progress down the road to profitability. Such thinking can go a long way toward helping you meet your goals as you plan sales strategies.

First of all, determine who you are and what you stand for. If you're not sure, take the time to sort it out. You will find that if you have a clear mission statement and know how you will act on your beliefs, you will be well on your way to operating a socially responsible company. Your decisions about what you will pay your employees and how they will be treated will be guided by your values. The quality of the products you sell and how those products are delivered to customers will be affected by your values. Your refund policy and product replacement policy, as well as how your customers are treated, will be driven by your values.

Being clear about your values will give you the courage to say no to a sale when your integrity as a businessperson could be compromised. In other words, your values will guide how you sell your products. You may have the greatest product in the world, but in the long run, if your actions don't support your product and what your business claims to be, it's only a matter of time before an even more fabulous product comes along and knocks you out of the market-place.

Integrating your values into your business proposition is critical in driving sales. Let your values guide your sales efforts. If you try to juggle and weigh each aspect of your sales efforts with your values, you may find yourself engaged in a balancing act that tips over on the wrong side of the scale. If you want growth and strong performance, no matter what your business's size, keep your sales firmly anchored by the values you established when you began your business.

Our next example focuses on a company that determined its core values right from the beginning and has continued to align each aspect of the business with these values—to extraordinary sales success.

## *Values-Centered Selling Nets Results*

Tom's of Maine got its start in 1968 when Tom and Kate Chappell decided to create and sell their own natural personal care products when they couldn't find such products in stores. From the start, the company has been guided by a commitment to "do what is right for our customers, employees, communities, and environment." This includes creating safe, effective natural products free of dyes, sweeteners, and preservatives; harvesting, processing, and packaging with respect for natural resources; not testing on animals or using animal ingredients; and donating 10 percent of its profits and 5 percent of its employees' paid time to charitable organizations.[14]

In 2006, the company was sold to corporate giant Colgate-Palmolive, a decision that created concern among people in the socially responsible camp. Some wondered if Tom's of Maine could maintain its strong values-driven integrity. On the company's Web site, the Chappells addressed such concerns by stating that Tom's would remain intact in Kennebunk, Maine (the sale was structured to give the Chappell family a minority ownership), and they have worked out an agreement that will preserve the character, spirit, and values of the company as it grows.[15]

Such a sale can have enormous ramifications—both for Tom's of Maine and for the product category it markets. If indeed the company's values can be retained, a larger segment of the population may be educated about the naturals market, given Colgate's wide, established distribution channels. And of course, the more sales Tom's of Maine generates, the more successful it becomes in promoting the benefits of operating as a values-centered business.

With all of that said, let's take a look at how Tom's of Maine has become the leader in the U.S. naturals market by focusing on its values. Tom O'Brien, chief operating officer for the company, says Tom's of Maine sets priorities and devises action plans that are based on what company executives believe is the right thing to do. They don't consider the company to be so much a "socially responsible company" as a values-centered company whose values just happen to be very socially responsible. "We don't say we're a toothpaste company that also holds these values. We say, 'These are the values that we believe in and here's how we're going to develop our business, both in toothpaste and deodorants or any other business that we're in.'" This, according to O'Brien, creates an integrated model that is key to strong sales.[16]

Acting as a values-centered business can enhance your sales efforts, but it also comes into play when you have to make tough decisions. O'Brien and Tom Chappell regularly make values-centered sales calls to other companies' executives. "We go in," explains O'Brien, "with the CEO or president of a retailer and have a discussion about our values. And what we do is we build charts and put our values on one side and put their values on another, and we go in to actually have a dialogue about 'Is there anything that we share in common, as it relates to values?'" The two men have walked out of such meetings with a real commitment from executives to be more environmentally and socially responsible. And they've also walked out empty-handed, so to speak. O'Brien says they tell executives when their values don't align. "We're not afraid to turn down business if they're asking us to do something that's inconsistent with who we are as a company."[17]

Clearly, selling with values has propelled Tom's of Maine to huge financial gains and enabled it to fulfill its commitment to "do the right thing." This "from the beginning" stewardship model has guided the company throughout its thirty-eight-year history and has made it a leader in the natural care industry.

*** 

Stories like these fill the socially responsible arena in today's ever-expanding marketplace. They are stories of companies that blend purpose and values-driven ideals with creativity to offer goods and services in a wide variety of ways. In this book we examine aspects of selling and distributing products that capitalize on innovative processes. Sometimes this means putting a new spin on an old technique or collaborating with another business to create a promotion, and added profits, for both companies. It can mean finding ways to treat your employees well and create a regular recognition program so they feel their contributions are appreciated. And although each area we cover in this book has its own unique features and "reasons to be," you will find that profitability starts by creating an integrated values system that complements and supports each aspect of your business.

As your company evolves, your vision must be central to everything you do. If you can keep sight of your vision, you may find achieving bigger and better sales is a wonderful, natural by-product.

## COLLECTIVE WISDOM

• **Determine your compelling story.** Let it guide your interactions with others—your sales force, your customers, your suppliers, your employees. Make sure they understand your story, and make a point of determining others' compelling stories and how your operation can benefit them as you develop sales strategies.

• **Serve your community with your actions.** If your vision has roots in benefiting your community, find ways to develop win-win situations that will improve your community while building stronger sales or distribution methods.

• **Expand your vision as new growth opportunities appear.** Look for alliances with others connected to your business that will have a positive impact on them as well as your sales.

• **Be patient as you make changes.** If you're transforming your business into a more socially responsible venture, remember that redefining who you are probably won't happen overnight. Let the changes you're making be a symbol of what you are and plan to become, and use these changes to drive your sales in new directions.

• **Determine your values early.** Know who and what you are as a business and as a business leader. As you devise new sales strategies and create new ways to distribute your products, your values will keep you on a steady course and help you through the rough times.

# 2

# Defining your market

## THE CREATIVE CHALLENGE: Determining who your customer is and how you can keep focusing on that customer

Birkenstock USA began as a seller of innovative, comfortable footwear—perhaps too innovative at the time. When founder Margot Fraser began trying to wholesale the funny-looking German-made sandals in the United States, no one wanted to give her the time of day. But she was wearing the sandals and knew how therapeutic and comfortable they were. She was convinced Americans with tired, aching feet who would appreciate them were out there—if only people had the chance to put them on. This notion propelled Margot to her first event (a health food store convention), where people could try the sandals for themselves. Store owners liked how the sandals felt and told their customers about them, and the Birkenstock brand soon began to show up on feet throughout the country.

In this chapter we'll take a look at several kinds of businesses and see how they ended up with their customer base and their sales strategies for reaching those customers. You may start a business with a clear idea of who the target customer is. For example, if you're making biodegradable diapers, you know right off the bat that your customers are people with young children and that you would be wasting huge amounts of money if you advertised your product to people who don't have children. However, if your product has a wider appeal or fits into multiple niche markets (e.g., environmental, skiing, general outdoor), you may have difficulty figuring out the best way to reach the ideal customer to make the most of your efforts and therefore increase sales. And you may find out that as your business grows, your customer base will also expand, which may present new issues or force you to consider taking different approaches to capturing this burgeoning market.

For this chapter we are calling our lessons Defining Strategies. Consider the situations illustrated and see if they can help you more accurately pinpoint your customers as well as design strategies to make the most of your sales efforts.

# DEFINING STRATEGY NUMBER ONE: Target a specific segment of the

# population, but be open to adjusting your strategy as your business grows.

If you have a good product designed for a specific type of customer, sales can build quickly just by targeting individuals in that group. However, nothing is wrong with expanding your customer base if you see that your product can easily carry over into other segments of the population.

One way to ensure a smooth flow into a new customer base is to plan from the beginning to expand into other demographics. To do this you must have a product or service that lends itself to such expansion, but if you take steps in the early stages to eventually broaden your reach, you'll be ready to take the appropriate measures to design new marketing materials, educate your sales staff, and create new distribution channels if necessary.

## *Expanding the Empowerment Opportunities*

Nadine Thompson knew when she created Warm Spirit with her partner, Daniel Wolf, that she would eventually want to sell her personal care products and offer the business opportunity to individuals outside the initial target group: African American women. As the New Hampshire-based company gains attention around the country and its sales force expands, Nadine will have momentum to broaden both the customer base and the sales force.

In the early stages of Warm Spirit, Nadine deliberately focused on the African American community. Everything the company did in the first six years targeted this particular demographic. Models featured in catalogs and promotional materials were usually black, and some products were formulated for black women's needs, such as the company's hair butter, which is traditionally used by women of color. Nadine first presented the company and its products at African American Women on Tour events.

Although Nadine wanted to present her new products and the Warm Spirit business opportunity specifically to African American women, she was also clear about the type of black women she wanted to reach: those who were middle-class and upwardly mobile. This focus was especially critical in the early stages of building the company since Nadine knew that this type of woman was needed to lead others in creating strong individual sales organizations. The African American Women on Tour events were the perfect venue since many of the women who attended were corporate executives or entrepreneurs already. Several of Warm Spirit's top consultants came from the relationships Nadine built at these events.

Today, Warm Spirit is attracting the attention of customers and entrepreneurs of other ethnicities, and Nadine hopes that this interest will continue to grow. Plans are underway to translate marketing materials into Spanish to better reach the Hispanic market, and Nadine is eager to work with Native Americans to develop new product formulations as well as see if she can create a business opportunity tailored specifically for them. The Caucasian market is also a large part of this expanded vision. Nadine has always made it clear to her consultants that she wanted to include the white market, and she feels the black consultants have been good about sharing the opportunity and products with their white friends and coworkers. Men are also joining the company, albeit in small numbers, which pleases Nadine.

Nadine had a clear vision about providing an opportunity and product for African American women when she and Daniel started the company. But they also knew from the beginning that even though they wanted to start there, that's not where they wanted to end up. With the future in mind, Nadine had both the white and black segments of the population in focus.

# DEFINING STRATEGY NUMBER TWO: Remain true to your original product concept and target customer while broadening your sales efforts.

As many entrepreneurs discover, an idea built around satisfying a personal need can often catapult a company into sizable sales. The trick is to maintain the focus behind the original idea as you expand your business and add products to your line. Once again, think ahead. Your original idea may be unique to the marketplace, but consider how you could eventually expand this concept when the time is right.

You may need to study market trends to see where your customers are headed in the future. You will also learn from your existing customers, suppliers, and distributors if you maintain open lines of communication. Study your own sales trends and learn from them. Is your product selling better in one part of the country than another? If so, why? If you have more than one package design, is one outselling the others? You may not have the budget for pricey research, but simple, constant communication and a look at your sales numbers can tell you volumes.

When you are ready to expand your product line, remain true to the concept that propelled you into business in the first place. You can keep your focus and build on this original concept when adding new products, which is what our next example demonstrates.

## Seeking All Thirst Quenchers

For Seth Goldman, who created Bethesda, Maryland-based Honest Tea with his friend and business school professor, Barry Nalebuff, creating a company that sold naturally brewed tea was simply a matter of quenching his thirst. It's a bit more complex than that, but the whole idea grew out of both men's desire to find a drink that wasn't loaded with sugars, like most colas, or wasn't tasteless, like bottled waters. A few years later, after Seth had finished business school, he concocted his own tea after a run and contacted Barry about starting their own tea beverage company. Barry had coincidentally recently returned from India, where he was analyzing the tea industry. Seth realized that if he was going to have his "perfect drink," he was going to have to make it himself. Barry suggested they use real tea leaves instead of the dust and fannings most American tea bottlers used, and they quickly settled on a name for their brand: Honest Tea.

The name resonated with Seth because he wanted to create a company that not only offered a pure, all-natural beverage but also created healthy and honest relationships with its customers, its suppliers, and the environment. The pair began lining up investors. Seth brewed batches of tea in his kitchen and carted thermoses of his beverage to potential stores, and soon the partners were satisfying the thirsts of people all over the country.[1]

Seth and Barry began by creating a tea that was made from real tea leaves and contained only a little sugar—something that differentiated their company in the marketplace and got sales rolling. However, their company evolved when Seth decided the next step should be creating an organic tea. Their first organic product was First Nation Peppermint, produced in 1999. Helping Honest Tea add an organic product to its lineup was the fact that tea plantations started switching to organic production, partly because of a pesticide scare that affected tea growers in the mid-1990s. In addition, in 2002, the U.S. Department of Agriculture launched an organic seal that began to appear on foods such as milk, fruits, vegetables, and meat. This seal gained credibility, which helped Honest Tea promote its organic product.[2] Honest Tea was also the first company to offer a Fair Trade Certified tea in 2003: Peach Oo-la-long Tea. Today, all Honest Tea products are organic, and the company is considered to be the best-selling and fastest-growing organic bottled tea company in the United States.[3]

New varieties of drinks are continually introduced, each maintaining the Honest Tea focus of "pure and natural." Today the company offers organic large-leaf tea bags and organic ready-to-drink tea and citrus quenchers in both glass and plastic bottles. Varieties include unsweetened teas, as well as Honest Ade fruit drinks and even Ten Calorie Tangerine Green, billed as the first organic diet beverage. In addition to carrying the certified organic label, all products are also certified kosher by the Orthodox Union, which gives the brand further appeal to a particular segment of the population.[4]

Honest Tea has remained true to its original focus of creating positive relationships with the company's suppliers and natural beverages that taste good without being loaded with sugar, even as it has added new varieties of beverages and expanded its customer base. The company is still committed to its socially responsible agenda, from considering the origin of the tea, how it is grown, and how the suppliers are paid and treated, to helping these suppliers build economic self-sufficiency and checking the quality of the product itself.[5] And the target customer is still someone who wants a great-tasting beverage that isn't loaded with sugar or artificial sweeteners. According to Seth, even celebrities like Whoopi

Goldberg now stock their refrigerators with Honest Tea.[6]

With sales growing each year, the company is finding that its attention to the thirsts of the world is paying off as it continues to expand and find new products to interest new thirsty customers.

# DEFINING STRATEGY NUMBER THREE: Find out where your potential customers are and go to them.

When you're getting started in a business, one-on-one product demonstrations can be a powerful pro-motional tool. Showing people—with enthusiasm—why they need your product is a great way to get your sales started and build brand awareness.

At first blush, such a prospect may seem overwhelm-ing. The initial step is to determine the types of events that best suit your product. For example, if your product serves a particular type of customer, then locate events that attract that type of individual. It takes time and usually booth expense to attend such events, so target your sales as carefully as possible. An ideal place to start is in your community since you won't have high travel costs. Farmers' markets are a good bet, as well as home shows, expos, and events related to certain areas of interest, such as homes, food, and outdoor recreation. If you have the budget, consider attending national trade or gift shows or other events that offer booth space for merchants. Such events are especially valuable if you want to wholesale your product to stores in a wide area.

Think about how you're going to attract attention to your booth so customers will listen to and watch your product demonstration. Samples are a great way to entice prospective buyers to check out your product. People love to receive "free stuff," and if you can give them a taste or feel or scent (whatever lends itself to sampling) of what you're selling, they will likely give you a few minutes of their time. And what if they like the sample but don't buy on the spot? Make sure they leave your booth with a business card or other information so they can order your product later.

Personality is also important. People like to know the person who is selling them a product. If it's hard for you to talk to strangers, practice until you can smile and talk comfortably. There is a fine line between being a "pushy" salesperson and one who is engaging and fun to talk with. Find that line and make sure people truly enjoy meeting you and learning about your product.

If sampling isn't appropriate for your product, think of innovative ways you can attract people to your booth. Can you create a simple game that will engage people and give them a chance to win a prize? Can you offer a chance to win one of your products by filling out a form (which also gives you follow-up and contact list information)? Can you create some form of entertainment that will attract attention?

Also consider the type of venue you're attending. If the event attracts individuals who are very interested in environmental issues, you might think of a way to tie in support of an environmental cause with the purchase of your product during the event. The important point is to understand the types of customers who will be walking by your booth and what you can do both to entice them to investigate your product and to then purchase it.

And finally, we remind you that follow-up is crucial when you are introducing a new product or service to prospective customers. Remember that they, like you, will get busy when they get home. They may even lose your business card or brochure or forget the name of your product. And while they may remember meeting you and seeing your product, it is up to you to remind them why they were interested and how your product will benefit them.

In the following example, we'll show you how one entrepreneur propelled her company into a multimillion-dollar operation by starting out with product demonstrations at an event tailored to her product.

## *So Many American Feet*

Like Seth Goldman and Barry Nalebuff, Margot Fraser of Birkenstock USA in Novato, California, found a way to fulfill a personal need with a product and decided that other people must have that same need. In Margot's case, her target market was feet—feet that hurt or were tired from walking or standing. Margot discovered the Birkenstock brand when she was in Germany in 1966. The company's sandals, developed by the grandson of Konrad Birkenstock (who had created a flexible arch support for shoes in 1902), were immensely comfortable and also alleviated the chronic foot pain Margot had endured for years. Inspired, she set out to import the footwear to the United States and sell it to other people who wanted comfortable shoes to wear.[7] "I thought, Oh, this is a fantastic product!" she says. "And look how many millions of feet there are in the United States."[8]

However, this was 1966, and the sandals were odd looking and completely foreign to American customers. Margot quickly learned that shoe stores did not share her enthusiasm for what she deemed was therapeutic footwear. With no real business plan or venture capital in hand, Margot was attempting to create a distribution network for the sandals based solely on her gut instinct that others would find them as necessary for comfort as she did. Her husband felt she should wholesale them instead of merely selling them to friends. But her first sales call to a shoe store lasted about two minutes when the owner told her he could never sell them. Since she lived in Santa Cruz, California, Margot next tried a friend of her husband's who was from Switzerland and owned a store in nearby Berkeley. She got an hour with this retailer, but the answer was the same: "This will never work."

Undaunted, Margot held fast to her belief that other people would fall in love with the funny-looking sandals if they got the chance to try them. Serendipity played a role next when a friend in the health food business suggested she attend a national convention of health food stores and show the sandals there. The year was 1967 and the convention was being held in San Francisco.

As we illustrated in our opening example, Margot's decision to take her unfamiliar footwear to potential customers rather than trying to draw them into a retail store is what catapulted her into a business success. "It was a lucky coincidence," recalls Margot. "But really the only way to do something is to be out in public, where people can see the product and you can tell them about it. And that's what started it."[9]

One of the store owners returned to Margot's booth on the last day of the convention. The woman had purchased a pair of the sandals and liked them so much she wanted three more pairs. "She said, 'You know, I think you really have something.'" Margot recalls.[10] The woman bought all three pairs in her size so if she couldn't sell them she could wear them herself. But the sandals sold and the woman turned out to be not only Margot's best customer but later her partner.

More customers were created as shoe stores began to realize how popular the brand was becoming in the United States. "There was this gradual branching out that started in' 73, but especially in' 74, shoe stores came all by themselves because either their customers told them about it and said, 'You know, you should really sell this product,' or they saw people coming out of health food stores with shoeboxes under their arm."[11]

At that time, the shoe stores were small, independent retailers. But another interesting phenomenon began to take shape that caused Margot's business to expand. Some people, mostly students who did not want to go into jobs in corporate America, decided they could make a living running Birkenstock shoe stores. The first shop opened in 1974, and the stores flourished.

Margot believes her lack of investors (the business was self-financed in the early stages) was a positive factor since it allowed the business to grow only slowly. "Certain things you just can't push," she states. Because she did not have large investment funding that would allow her to advertise the footwear, Margot had to continue to show the sandals to potential customers at health fairs and other venues so they could actually see the product, touch it, and try it out. She feels the customers themselves were the best advocates for the product. "That's still very much the scene in stores nowadays. When there is a new customer in the store who doesn't quite under-stand the shoes, then there's usually somebody who says, 'Oh, yes, I've worn them for ten years and couldn't be without them.' So it's more the intimate knowledge of the product that sells it to the next person."[12] And this personal, one-on-one contact with satisfied customers who gave word-of-mouth endorsements is what turned Birkenstock USA into a successful, multimillion-dollar business.

# DEFINING STRATEGY NUMBER FOUR: Don't be afraid to embrace new customers who seem outside your target market.

Open your mind and your sales prospects to customers you may have previously ignored—or just never considered. Although having a clear idea of your ideal customer is important, remember that your product or service may attract customers you'd never considered before—or even had dismissed as unlikely prospects.

You created your business because you felt a need existed for your product. Perhaps this need has roots of a personal nature, or you carefully researched trends and saw an overwhelming consumer need no one else was meeting. Whatever the case, you should have a pretty good idea of who your target customer is.

We've discussed planning to expand your customer base as your business grows and following the natural evolution of your product's position in the marketplace. But what about those customers you never expected to attract? If they aren't part of your sales game plan and you aren't willing to consider the sales opportunities they present, you may find yourself conveniently ignoring them—much to your detriment.

Here's an example of a company that is attracting customers from opposite ends of the demographic spectrum, much to the delight of its founders.

# Connecting to the "Moved and Shaken"

For a product like Birkenstock footwear, a business owner soon learns the value of getting to know the target audience in order to boost sales. Other businesses, however, tend to cast a much wider net, and sometimes the customers turn out to be some-what surprising. Such is the case for Link TV, a nonprofit broadcast entity headquartered in San Francisco, California, that is dedicated to providing Americans with global perspectives on news, events, and culture. Launched in December 1999 on DirecTV and added to EchoStar's DISH Network a few weeks later, Link TV is the brainchild of independent television producer Kim Spencer and his partners, Jack Willis and David Michaelis.[13] Although Kim and his partners were careful not to give Link TV any sort of political stance of its own, they were determined not to follow what is broadcast in the conventional media. "We're here to provide alternatives that wouldn't be available if we didn't exist," explains Kim.[14]

This desire to be an alternative voice and television channel was sparked when international producer Kim noticed the huge number of quality programs pro-duced overseas that never made it before U.S. audi-ences. American broadcast decision makers deemed such programs of no interest to their audiences, but

Kim didn't believe that. He refused to listen to the so-called industry experts who felt they knew what the American public wanted (and viewpoints from other parts of the world were not it). So the trio proceeded, going on the air with a minuscule $3 million in grants (as compared to the $15 to $20 million they were told they would need to get off the ground).[15]

The mission of Link TV is to broadcast programs that engage, educate, and activate viewers to become involved in the world. The programs are designed to provide a unique perspective on international news, current events, and diverse cultures and to present issues not often covered in the U.S. media. Link TV's goal is to connect American viewers with the people at the heart of breaking events, the organizations in the forefront of social change, and the cultures of an increasingly global community. One of the channel's commitments is to give a voice to those without a voice—to connect viewers not only to the "movers and shakers" but also to the "moved and shaken." In addition, Link TV offers program trailers and information on its Web site so viewers can access tools that will enable them to take action on social issues. The network has the flavor of PBS with its noncommercial format, pledge drives, and underwriting. However, it does not accept corporate underwriting (funding from companies) for programming.[16]

One of the network's most popular programs, *Mosaic: World News from the Middle East,* distills news reports  from thirty Middle Eastern television outlets and presents portions translated into English but not censored. The program earned Link TV a prestigious George Foster Peabody Award in 2005. Not only is the program popular with the general public, it also seems to have a loyal following among those in the White House and U.S. State Department. Kim says the White House Communications Office calls Link TV to find out if the time of the show is changed. "You would think the CIA would do their monitoring for them," adds Kim, "but we're happy to help."[17]

One would think a television network that presents world views and international slants on stories affecting the American public would garner a fairly  liberal following. However, according to Kim, the network really has no target demographic; viewers range from those over sixty to Gen Xers who appreciate the network's global hip-hop music.[18] And what about that tricky divider called politics? Even though Kim admits that Link TV has a lot of viewers he would call "cultural creatives" or "progressives" and who do not as a rule watch mainstream media, he's done some research and discovered that in the 2004 election, Link TV viewers' political leanings weren't all that lopsided: 42 percent voted for Kerry and 31 percent voted for Bush. "We are very happy with that," he adds, "because it means we're reaching people who are looking for new ideas and listening. We're not just presenting one point of view."[19]

Although the majority of Link TV's funding comes from foundations, 20 percent is donated by viewers through individual contributions. The average contribution is high—$155 as compared to public television's $77[20]—a factor Kim feels may be because viewers are so passionate and understand the importance of the network's mission.[21]

Kim knows he needs to continually think about ways to keep viewers actively involved monetarily. "People are contributing to Link because of its social purpose," he says. "There's no direct financial benefit." However, after about two years of operation, and again following the model of public television, the network did start to offer premiums, or gifts, as incentives to get people to contribute. And this strategy takes continued fine-tuning as well. "We have to constantly upgrade what we're doing and find new ways to present what we're about." Kim has found that focusing the on-air pitches has been a help in boosting donations. "We've been focusing a lot on theme nights, where we've been particularly successful."[22]

As this example shows, you need to continually review your sales strategies and efforts to reach out to your customers to create new and larger sales. Maybe this means coming up with new product launches so something "fresh" is always in the product pipeline or creating a promotion that attracts attention—among your established customers as well as among new individuals you might not have thought about before.

# DEFINING STRATEGY NUMBER FIVE: Connect with retailers that sell to your end consumer.

Creating effective sales strategies is often like putting a puzzle together. You must assemble all the pieces so the end result is both pleasing and tightly connected. You may want to think about factors such as who your suppliers are and whether their goals align with yours and your customers' interests. Or can you connect with your customers in ways that will build interest in your mission as well as in your product?

An important element of this puzzle and selling your product is establishing a strong connection with those to whom you are wholesaling. This is a way for you to strengthen your sales on two levels: to the retailer and to the end consumer. It's worth repeating that strong, long-term sales depend on much more than just exchanging money for a product, even if it's a high quality product that is in demand. If you get to know the retailers who are in turn creating connections with your end consumer, you can develop relationships that will carry you through sales slumps, give you new ideas for improving your product, and support you when a challenge occurs (e.g., a shipment fails to arrive on time). As you build your business and develop your distribution channels, connecting to your retailers will be an essential part of your business puzzle and one that gives you a solid, satisfying picture in the end.

Our final example is a business that has a strong history of connecting to build sales in a niche market.

## *"Store Busting" Gets Results*

Dan Storper of Putumayo World Music, based in New York City, discovered early in building his business that people-to-people contact was key to promoting his CDs. Although he initially collaborated with Rhino Records to get the CDs into mainstream record stores, he focused on nontraditional stores, or the "specialty" market. When sales to record stores didn't meet Rhino's expectations, a year later Dan "took over the whole shebang." He found a distributor to sell to record stores and in 1996 began to sell his music compilations to international markets. But he still worked the specialty stores and sold to individual retailers. Today in the United States, about 60 percent of Putumayo World Music's sales come from specialty stores and 40 percent from record stores. In Europe the split is about 50-50. "We wouldn't have been in this business without the specialty stores," adds Dan.[23]

Dan and his business partner, Michael Kraus, discovered that the way to sell their world music CDs was by setting up booths at trade shows. "So it was really just trying to convince them that there was logic for them to start selling music and then the idea that they'd make additional money from doing this because it's great music to play in the stores." Dan was familiar with these small, specialty stores because they had been carrying his Putumayo clothing in his previous business, and he was comfortable with the idea of selling relatively small quantities.[24]

"My biggest focus is really connecting the dots with both retailers and consumers," he explains. "So I'm very much somebody who believes not just in doing trade shows but in going out and visiting stores." Dan estimates that he's visited thousands of retailers and accounts because it gives him a better sense of what the stores need and want. He calls this "store busting" and considers it to be a huge part of what he does. And by getting to know the stores that carry his music and by offering contests and special events, Dan is learning how to please and continue to sell his product to his customers.[25]

Dan's efforts to visit the stores that carry his music are similar to the ways that companies like Warm

Spirit and Birkenstock first attracted attention to their products. However, in Putumayo's case, Dan felt a need to connect directly with the retailers in their establishments because he wanted to know what the stores looked like, how they operated, and what kind of customer they attracted. In this way he could create a better connection between his music and the stores that carried his product.

By understanding both the stores' needs and his end consumers' needs, he can create a better product that fits those needs—which means more sales.

*** 

As the examples in this chapter illustrate, you can reach your target customer and expand your customer base in many ways as your business grows. One of the most important elements is to determine how your product will benefit your customers and tie that benefit into your outreach efforts. But first and foremost, define whom you are trying to reach and plan your sales and distribution strategies around this point. As your business grows, you can then consider new products or new benefits that will allow you to sell to new customers.

# COLLECTIVE WISDOM

- **Make room for "others."** Your product may initially fit a specific niche market, but consider ways you can eventually broaden your customer base as your business grows. Look down the road—in the early planning stages—and think about how you might offer additional benefits that will attract a new segment of the population.

- **Focus on your initial product mission.** As you create new products, stay true to your initial product vision. If, for example, your business was founded on creating an organic product, remain true to this ideal as you develop new products.

- **Find your customers.** Go to your customers and follow up with those you meet. You can find many events, often close to home, where you can present your product and explain its benefits. Word-of-mouth advertising, especially when you're starting out, can be a powerful sales tool. Consider local home shows, health fairs, festivals, business conferences with attendees who match your target customer, and community events, as well as larger trade shows and national conferences.

- **Keep an open mind.** Remember that your product may wind up appealing to customers you never considered in the early planning stages. Be willing to explore new avenues for expansion and ways to best serve these new customers.

• **Connect.** Develop relationships with those who are selling your product. If you sell to retail stores, find out what the retailers like about your product and how it enhances their business. Visit the stores as often as you can and get a true feel for their operations. If you can't visit the stores, call them periodically. Again, listen to the retailers' feedback and the comments they are willing to share with you about their customers' reactions to your product.

# 3

# Building strong distribution channels

## THE CREATIVE CHALLENGE: Finding innovative ways to ensure your products are in the outlets best designed to reach your customers

For twenty-one years, French Meadow Bakery's Lynn Gordon has "lived" in grocery stores. Why? Because that's how she's learned what the trends are and who shops in each store. Once she's done that, she can determine which of her products will sell in those stores. Lynn's family is used to her making the grocery store rounds on vacations since the bakery founder is always trying to figure out how to get her products into more customers' hands. She writes notes to store managers who are not carrying French Meadow products to let them know that as a customer—not as the company owner—she wishes they'd carry the brand. Lynn estimates she's written close to 2,000 notes over the years. She's never flinched about this guerilla approach to encouraging stores to stock French Meadow because she believes wholeheartedly in the quality and taste of her products and knows they'll sell and customers will love them. And she does it because "if a customer asks, the buyer at the store listens."[1]

Once you've determined who your target customer is, you need to figure out how to get your product to this ideal customer. If you're wholesaling to retailers, your first concern is developing effective distribution channels so your product is placed in stores where your end customer will see it. If you're selling directly to customers, you need to have a system in place so your product can be shipped in a timely fashion to your own store or to your customers.

A strong distribution channel is critical to your sales and growth as a company. In this chapter we'll give you some examples of companies that have created good relationships with their distributors or found creative ways to get their products to their customers themselves.

Creating effective distribution channels involves a number of factors: developing relationships with those who are carrying your product; using shipping methods that get your product to the store quickly and without damage; meeting promised deadlines; and delivering a high-quality, uniform product. You will have to make sure each of these elements is well thought out and that you maintain consistency in each area as your business grows.

If you are wholesaling to retailers, you have to convince these retailers that their customers will want your product. One way you can do this is by selling the value of your product to the end customer. An example of this strategy is holding a special in-store promotion that highlights your product or educates the store's customers about your product or socially responsible mission.

However you put your product into customers' hands, you can incorporate the following Distribution Strategies into your operation to help you with this very important part of building a successful business and continued strong sales.

# DISTRIBUTION STRATEGY NUMBER ONE: Know your distribution channels and target your efforts to meet the needs of each.

Your business may rely on several different ways to get your product to your customers. You may have a retail store of your own with online, telephone, and catalog/mail-order capabilities, as well as wholesale your product to other retailers. To be able to put your product into the hands of your customers by using all of these methods, you need to adapt your sales efforts, product lines, and shipping methods accordingly. This means thoroughly understanding the needs of each of these sales and distribution channels.

Keep in mind the nature of your sales for each. In other words, who is purchasing through each channel, what are they buying, and why are they buying it? You may find that you are selling to different departments within the same organization. Each department may require a different product and a different shipping method, and you may need a different approach when developing a relationship with each department buyer.

Establishing a strong relationship with a distributor is a critical first step. However, products often find new avenues of distribution, and you will have to consider new options as they appear. For example, if you are selling a product to a store for placement on its shelves and suddenly the store manager asks if you can create custom-made gift baskets that customers can order in advance, ask yourself if you can find a way to meet this demand and still maintain the integrity of your brand.

Our next entrepreneur learned that taking her story directly to store buyers could get her toe in the door of building a strong distribution network.

# Lessons with the Buyers

Kunmi Oluleye of Atlanta-based Sheba Foods had an idea that kept surfacing in her mind, and eventually she acted on it, using her faith, belief in herself, and instincts to keep it rolling. A native of Nigeria, she had been preparing African food for years for her family, and she often froze it to be reheated later. She decided to approach grocery stores about carrying her frozen African food—before she developed any packaging. When a supermarket executive said yes, he'd buy her products, Kunmi was forced to quickly learn more about what was involved in getting her products into stores and making sure they sold. Like Lynn Gordon of French Meadow Bakery, she put in aisle time to determine what kinds of products were on the shelves, how she should design her packaging, what her price point should be, and any other requirements that would help sell her products. Once she knew how to best present her products, she approached the store buyers and followed up with them. All of this she calls "lessons with the buyers."[2]

Once Sheba Foods is in a store, Kunmi often does product demonstrations and samplings to help promote sales. At Whole Foods, a natural food giant and a distribution channel Kunmi recently added, she will be teaching a cooking class. The entrepreneur also has her own store in Atlanta, where she tests new products before taking them to supermarkets. And she uses the Internet to showcase her line and sell products.

Determined to make a profit from the beginning, Kunmi has always built in at least a small profit, and she discounts the standard notion that a new business can't be profitable for the first three years. She tries to price on the high side and lets buyers tell her if they think her products are too expensive.

Kunmi has big plans for Sheba Foods. She wants to take the company nationwide in the next eighteen months, and she hopes to open a big supermarket that will feature everything, from food and apparel to music, pertaining to the varied African cultures. In addition, she wants to open "African food, fast" restaurants all over the country ("There's nothing fast food about African food," she explains), and in nine years she intends to go public.[3]

Kunmi has traveled her entrepreneurial road by adhering to two important philosophies. First, she listens to her instincts and doesn't let anyone tell her that she can't do something. "When you tell me, 'Kunmi, you can't do this. You're going to fail at this,' then that is where the adrenaline comes from that says, 'Watch me prove you wrong!'" she explains. And second, she believes a person must get comfortable with failure and have an exit plan when things don't work out as planned.[4] With Sheba Foods already making appearances throughout the eastern United States, Kunmi is well on her way to proving any disbelievers wrong.

## DISTRIBUTION STRATEGY NUMBER TWO: Make sure your values are aligned with the values of those who are selling your product.

You might be tempted to put your product anywhere a potential customer is located, especially when you're starting out and trying to build sales and gain a name for your brand. However, as a socially responsible company, your brand is directly connected to your company's actions and to your core values. This means that you need to develop relationships with distributors who share your values and will support your mission and build respect for what you stand for as a socially responsible company.

Kellie McElhaney of the Center for Responsible Business believes that when you're trying to get into the supply chain, the challenge is utilizing your commitment to corporate social responsibility (CSR) as it relates to trust. "In so many people's minds," she says, "a company or leader who's committed to CSR is viewed as more trustworthy, and we all want to do business with trustworthy business partners."

Kellie feels that you must consider two important points when attempting to get your product into the distribution channel. First, establish yourself as a trusted business partner with a quality brand and a reputation for delivering on what you say you'll deliver on. And second, keep your sustainability or CSR message short and to the point, and then train the distributor about how to talk to your end consumer about it.[5]

To demonstrate this "short and to the point" messaging, Kellie cites a California vineyard that has developed a distributor kit that provides a little bit of information about its organic growing process. The vineyard is also creating a hang tag for its bottles so the consumer can see the wine's benefits as an organic product. By developing the CSR messaging and making it clearly visible on the product, the vineyard is promoting its social responsibility and also  helping the distributor to look good because it is carrying a product that has a socially responsible track record.[6]

In our next example, we show how a company committed to the triple bottom line of people, planet, and profits and operating under the philosophy that it will "only be successful if behind every product we share with you, are countless ways in which the lives of those who grew it, harvested it, produced it, and brought it to you are affected for the good"[7] is

getting its products into stores and educating consumers about its message.

## Conscious Goods and Conscious Actions

Kopali Organics is a fair-commerce organic specialty food company that was founded in 2004 at Punta Mona, an off-the-grid educational farm and sustainability center in the rainforest of Costa Rica. Founders Zak Zaidman and Stephen Brooks feel one of the major threats to people's health and the health of the planet is large-scale chemical agriculture—a situation they witnessed firsthand in Costa Rica. With Kopali, they wanted to create bridges between small organic farmers and the growing market of conscious consumers.[8]

Zak feels they are participating in a trend of total transparency—a transparent chain from the consumer all the way to where the product originated. In other words, everybody knows everybody else and how they operate, and they are all connected by a chain of actions that is designed to be good for everyone. Kopali actually got started when Zak and Stephen realized that most of the bananas farmed in Costa Rica for U.S. consumption are grown using tremendous amounts of pesticides, herbicides, and chemical fertilizers that create a long history of death and destruction. When they found a few farmers who were still growing crops in sustainable ways, they wanted to help them sell their products in the international marketplace since these farmers could never compete with large growers on their own.

The founders discovered a product common to Costa Rica but unknown in the United States—banana vinegar, made from bananas that get too ripe. The vinegar is a staple in Costa Rican kitchens. A non-governmental organization (NGO) had previously established certification cooperatives in the region for farmers who were growing crops organically and had already set up a factory for producing the vinegar. Zak and Stephen were aware that farmers now receive only about 5 percent of a crop's value, as compared to 95 percent in the past. So their goal was to allow these local farmers to profit from this value-added, nonperishable product they were producing. In the process, they wanted to share these farmers' wisdom for benefiting humanity with customers in other parts of the world and promote this wisdom and the benefits of organic farming.

To get Kopali's products into the U.S. market, Zak and Stephen approached Whole Foods, and, according to Zak, they literally sat on the same side of the table and hammered out an equitable way to put Kopali products into the chain's stores by using a centralized warehouse. Because Kopali's founders had a clear agenda about their products and their mission, it made sense for them to distribute their products through a natural food chain like Whole Foods.

Key to Kopali's success, Zak feels, is telling people what they need to know and continuing to promote the company's mission-oriented work. The Kopali team promotes the company with Conscious Goods Caravan Tours featuring a 100 percent vegetable-oil-fueled bus. The team members take their conscious lifestyle message and products across the country, promoting the importance of organic agriculture, fair commerce, renewable energies, and other sustainable solutions. They also created a television program that premiered on the Travel Channel and are producing documentaries and other videos to promote their cause and the farmers' products.

But whatever they do, from getting their products into more and more stores to generating broader brand awareness, their story is what drives their actions: "The story that we act behind is these small farmers that are the holdouts," explains Zak, "growing food sustainably, who are our friends, who are people that we know and really love and are real heroes."[9]

# DISTRIBUTION STRATEGY NUMBER THREE: Believe in your product and

# be bold about promoting it wherever you are.

Throughout this book you will read about business leaders who have become successful because they put their passion for their mission and their product behind their actions as businesspeople. Passion carries over into many realms in the business world—the publicity you receive, the attitude you foster among your workforce, your ability to attract investors, the actual sales you generate in dealing with customers. It also is important when you are setting up your distribution channels. Even once you've gotten your product distributed, you may have to work at promoting your product to your distributors or to your end consumer.

This point was illustrated in our opening example when we explained how Lynn Gordon visits grocery stores to learn about trends and the stores' customers and then lets the stores know she would like them to carry French Meadow Bakery products. As Lynn points out, stores listen to customers. Lynn's approach is a form of word-of-mouth advertising, which, of course, is a powerful tool in building brand identity, putting products on shelves, and creating interest among consumers.

When it comes to food products, personal testimonials and word-of-mouth "publicity" are extremely effective.

Think about it—how many times have you tried a new restaurant because a friend raved about it or you read an especially glowing review by the local food critic? Since food is a product that offers not only sustenance but pleasure, reaching customers on a visceral level can be very important when you're building distribution channels to add more customers. And while your goal may be to promote the health benefits of your product and overall socially responsible aspects of your business, you first must reach customers where they really "get" it. And in the case of food, that's often how it tastes and how it makes a person feel.

Kellie McElhaney has discovered this fact in her work with socially responsible companies that market health-conscious products. She feels the first step in building sales is connecting with customers on this visceral level—convincing them that the products are good for them to put in their bodies. Once they have accepted this idea, they tend to be much more receptive to broader socially responsible actions, such as caring for the environment and creating healthier growing conditions. "It's got to pass through the actual physical being of a consumer first," Kellie says.[10]

This takes us back to being passionate about your product. If you know you have a terrific product that will somehow benefit people, sharing this passion and enthusiasm with everyone you encounter can help convince people that your product is worth trying. If they like your product and what it does for them, they are going to be more receptive to the rest of your message. Kellie adds that while corporate socially responsible messaging is effective and can definitely differentiate your product (to distributors as well as your end customer), it does not stand alone. It has to be combined with more traditional sales techniques, such as high quality and competitive pricing.[11]

As our next example shows, Lynn Gordon carries her guerilla approach to marketing beyond the grocery stores where she wants her products to be sold. For years she has made a point to tout the benefits and taste of her products directly to customers. Her children may wince when their mother starts talking, but her technique is effective and has helped to make French Meadow Bakery a powerhouse in the organic bread category.

## *Successful in Spite of Themselves*

Lynn never expected to create a highly successful business. She just loved to make bread and figured she could do something she loved and eke out a living, and all would be well. But when her breads and sweet goods and later sandwiches and soups started to create a clamor and a growing demand, she realized that she and business partner Steve Shapiro had a business and products with wide appeal.

Like many great success stories, Lynn's journey began simply. In 1985 she was a macrobiotic teacher who decided to bake her own yeast-free, organic bread and make it available on a wholesale basis in Minneapolis, where she lived and worked. Once people in the neighborhood where the bakery was located got a whiff of the freshly baked bread, they began begging Lynn to open a retail store. Lynn gave in, got out her family recipes, and threw together "on a dime" French Meadow's Minneapolis cafe. She was so convinced that the cafe wouldn't attract any attention, she told Steve they wouldn't need a cash register—the box they took to the farmers' market would be fine. But people poured in, and Lynn was soon yelling for someone to find a cash register. According to Lynn, she and Steve were "successful in spite of them-selves." The place quickly became one of the city's hot spots—it even attracts Hollywood celebrities who want natural, organic fare when they're in town. Lynn also says the cafe is where all of the natural food industry executives do their "wheeling and dealing." Even Social Venture Network took root in the French Meadow Bakery & Cafe.

Since it opened, French Meadow Bakery has grown considerably, with two locations at the Minneapo-lis/Saint Paul airport and an organic wine and martini bar that is slated to open in December 2006. French Meadow's presence at the airport led to a partnership with the SuperValu grocery chain's Sunflower Market, which is featuring the bakery in stores in Broad Ripple, Indiana; Chicago; and Columbus, Ohio. According to Lynn, plans are to open French Meadow bakeries in 100 Sunflower Markets around the country. The brand also can be found in the specialty, frozen, and refrigerated sections of major grocery stores nationwide. In addition, Lynn and Steve recently completed negotiations with a strategic partner that will enable French Meadow to expand even further. According to Lynn, this alliance will help her with day-to-day operations that aren't her strengths, such as managing, distributing, and building profit margins, and allow her to focus on aspects of the business where she excels: developing new products, being creative, and continuing her guerilla merchandise marketing techniques.

The airport cafes were the springboard for French Meadow's expansion via Sunflower Market locations. SuperValu executives saw the cafe, were impressed with it, and wanted to add French Meadow bakeries to their Sunflower Markets. Adding the airport as a distribution channel resulted from a combination of the hard work Lynn and Steve had put into their operation over the years, the quality products they had developed, and good old serendipity. Steve had heard that the airport was interested in adding local vendors as retailers, and on the day of a large meeting to introduce the concept, he told Lynn to get over there. Just returning from a trip, she arrived at the meeting late but did manage to get her business card to three people, one of whom was a French Meadow fan. A deal was reached, and the first airport French Meadow Bakery & Cafe opened in April 2005.

Now, about her guerilla marketing. If you're with Lynn at one of her cafes or shopping with her in a grocery where her products are sold, be prepared to witness a passionate entrepreneur in action. And pay attention because you will learn how she has turned French Meadow into a multimillion-dollar operation. "I'm extremely passionate and extremely tenacious," she says. "I never give up. I never stop believing in myself."[12]

When she's at the freezer section of the grocery and sees customers trying to decide what to select, she will fill her cart with French Meadow products and let those around her know why. "I pick up my bread and I put it in my cart and I say, 'Well, this one's amazing. My whole family eats it! We just love this bread.' And I leave a store and I've sold the whole freezer door."[13] This tactic does two things for French Meadow. One, it creates new customers. Two, it empties the freezer shelf. Will the store buyer notice this second fact? You bet, and this will help strengthen Lynn's relationship with that distributor.

Lynn is also a master at promoting her products in her cafes. Given the opportunity (and Lynn always finds one), she will rave about the sandwiches or bread or whatever a customer might be considering. A recent exchange at the airport cafe went like this: "A lady said she's waiting for a sandwich, and then I said, 'Oh my God, they're the best chicken sandwiches. You know it's organic, don't you?' And she said, 'No,' and I said, 'Oh, we always eat here.' And then another lady chimed in, 'Oh, you're kidding. What else do you recommend?'"[14]

Lynn's honest enthusiasm for her products persuades people to try her recommendations—and no doubt, keep coming back. Friends have laughingly called her tactics "shameless," but Lynn believes too strongly in the quality of her products to ever stop. "I do it all the time, wherever I am," she adds.[15]

# DISTRIBUTION STRATEGY NUMBER FOUR: Differentiate your product so it will stand out to retailers.

Differentiating your product is critical in a world where new products are constantly being launched and thrust upon consumers. You have probably addressed this issue from the very start of your business. If you're selling directly to your end customer, you know your product must stand out and offer a benefit to that customer. Differentiation can entail many factors: quality, ingredients, who makes your product, how it affects the environment, how it benefits your suppliers—the list could go on and on.

When you are wholesaling and trying to get your product into distribution channels, you must also consider ways to differentiate your product so it will attract buyers' attention and keep them reordering. Even though some of the same factors apply as when you're selling directly to consumers, in this case you may be competing for shelf space in a sea of products similar to yours. Or you may be introducing a product that is unfamiliar to the distributor and therefore is an unknown commodity when it comes to how it will sell.

Here we present an example of a product line that gained a foothold in a distribution channel and maintained it as its category *and* the industry grew.

## *Better-Tasting Products*

Imagine Foods, now part of the Hain Celestial Group of Melville, New York, and created in 1982 by Robert Nissenbaum and a partner, introduced Rice Dream and Soy Dream to consumers back when such dairy alternative products were largely unknown. In the eighties, according to Robert, natural food stores didn't even carry dairy products, so there wasn't much of a demand to carry dairy alternatives in those stores. And groceries didn't carry natural foods at all back then. However, some consumers had a need for such products because of dairy allergies or other concerns. Soy products were just beginning to be introduced, but the taste left a lot to be desired. And the natural food industry offered few prepared products, especially prepared foods that you'd enjoy eating. Enter Imagine's Rice Dream, Soy Dream, and frozen nondairy desserts and shelf-stable soups, which became popular because they tasted really good.

"Imagine Foods became really successful and known because we made better-quality, better-tasting prepared food products," explains Robert. This was the differentiator that got the brand shelf space in stores, especially Whole Foods, which Robert started selling to before the grocer became a national chain. Because Imagine's products were always some of the bestselling products in the entire natural food category, they evolved with Whole Foods as the grocer began to expand around the country. Robert credits this industry giant's success in the natural food category with influencing mainstream groceries to begin carrying natural foods, which helped everyone who was making and marketing such products.[16]

Innovation in the form of a better-tasting product is what propelled Imagine Foods to a top-selling spot in the natural food category. Once it had a leading position in the category, it was easy for the company to keep growing as the entire industry expanded. Robert sold the company in 2004, but today the nondairy beverages and soups are still ranked as best sellers. "We were definitely one of the companies that started raising the bar for the quality of products that were out there," adds Robert. And quality made all the difference for this successful entrepreneur.[17]

# DISTRIBUTION STRATEGY NUMBER FIVE: Make it easy for your customers to buy and receive your product, as well as promote it to others.

Depending on your type of business, distributing your products may be as simple as getting your product from the manufacturer (which may be you) to your customer. You don't wholesale to retailers, so you avoid the middleman. You probably have a Web site and use it to provide information about your product and your mission. You may even have an online ordering system set up.

However your business is organized, it's important that you simplify the way your customers obtain your product. And if your customers themselves are instrumental in getting you more business, be sure to create a reward system that will encourage this action. You may want to build the cost of such a system into your operation from the beginning so it won't become a budget item you can't handle in the long run.

# No Stale Bread

Small Potatoes Urban Delivery (SPUD), based in Vancouver, British Columbia, started with a great idea and four employees that initially delivered to nine customers. Today the growing company delivers grocery items to over 6,000 customers and is branching out to the United States. It has streamlined its operation by making smart use of the Internet and builds increased distribution by developing strong relationships with its customers.

Key to SPUD's success, according to president and CEO David Van Seters, is the fact that customers don't have to read the labels when they order products through the grocery home delivery service. "It's that peace of mind," he says, "that they know if it's on our Web site, it's going to be okay."[18] In other words, SPUD customers know that the groceries they order are wholesome, usually locally grown and organic, and free of harmful ingredients.

SPUD's growth has taken an interesting route, and traditional mass advertising hasn't played a significant role. To get his distribution process up and running (SPUD sells and delivers directly to customers), David mailed flyers that educated people about the environmental, social, and personal economic benefits of having their groceries delivered. This meant pointing out the fossil fuel savings (one small truck can deliver 100 orders, which David compares to emptying a parking lot as well as cutting back on traffic congestion); the time savings a person enjoys by not spending the average ninety minutes a week grocery shopping; the money saved by not buying gas to drive to the grocery; and the quality of the products, which include fresh and organic produce. (Food is brought to SPUD's warehouse—mostly from local growers and suppliers—and delivered to customers within twenty-four hours, so they never have so much as day-old bread.)

One reason flyers work so well is because the company can target the audience geographically. If it has an area where SPUD can add customers, it can put out flyers in specific neighborhoods to build up the route. If SPUD did general advertising, it might end up with an oversized route and have to split it, which could create challenges in handling the deliveries. SPUD's customers themselves are also responsible for the company's growth. "Word of mouth is the number one way that we get customers," adds David. Supporting this customer-to-customer approach toward increasing sales is SPUD's generous customer-referral rebate program. Every customer's invoice has a coupon at the bottom that can be given to a friend for a discount off the first four orders. In addition, the person giving the referral also receives a discount. "I think we're probably closing in on 50 percent of our new customers coming from customer referrals," says David.[19]

The Internet also plays a major role in moving the business forward. Customers order online, pay online, and can even request products that SPUD doesn't currently carry. They can also go to the Web site and find out the distance every product travels to get to SPUD's warehouse (one-third the average distance compared to a conventional grocery or natural food store).

The folks at SPUD also use ingenuity in promoting the business and its multiple benefits. One Halloween they held a wake for a shopping cart, which had "died" because SPUD customers order online. They went through downtown with a gigantic coffin containing the shopping cart, ending up at the Vancouver Art Gallery, where they read a eulogy for the poor, deceased cart.[20]

Not only have all of these actions helped SPUD add customers and new distribution channels throughout four regions of North America, but they have helped the company gain valuable publicity in the media. And that helps David educate more and more people about the benefits of using SPUD to buy groceries, which adds up to increased sales and profitability—no small potatoes in the business world.

## DISTRIBUTION STRATEGY NUMBER SIX: Be willing to adapt your business to new distribution opportunities.

To put it simply, be flexible and open your mind to new possibilities about getting your products to your customers. Throughout your company's growth, you will encounter situations that may, at first glance, appear to be insurmountable challenges. If you can remain calm and look at the situation from all angles, you may discover an innovative approach that gives you a competitive edge in the marketplace.

You will also discover that innovation may surface in unlikely ways—through an employee suggestion, from a customer, via happenstance that forces you to look at your business in a new light. However it arrives, we encourage you to weigh the situation carefully and imagine where it could take you.

In considering new distribution opportunities, you may have to come up with new packaging, new shipping methods, or even a new formula if a potential distributor is interested in your product but has certain requirements. Your job is to determine whether making the changes will be cost effective and offer significant growth in the future. If you've created a strong relationship with the distributor, he may work with you about making the changes he needs in order to sell your product. For example, maybe he will allow you to sell a new design on a trial basis until both of you determine if it will be popular.

The next example shows how two entrepreneurs' flexibility in adapting their business when a problem developed has been instrumental to their success.

## What Are We Going to Do with All This Lettuce?

Myra and Drew Goodman found themselves in a quandary when the chef who had been buying their organic lettuce suddenly left town and the new chef told them he had his own supplier. Organic farming entrepreneurs in Carmel Valley, California, the young couple had a surplus of lettuce to sell and suddenly no buyer. The year was 1984, and the Goodmans were teaching themselves organic farming on their two and a half acres of land. They had already learned how to grow the farm's raspberry crop organically and were venturing into other produce, even though many in the area were telling them they were nuts. According to Samantha Cabaluna, senior marketing manager for Earthbound Farm, the couple were determined to follow their intuition. "They just had this intuitive gut reaction," she says, "and back then, before the Internet, they thought there's got to be a better way to do this. And they just started digging around and found *Rodale's Encyclopedia of Organic Gardening,* which was, of course, the bible. And they just said, 'Well, let's go for it!' And everybody told them they were insane."[21]

The farms were big in that part of the country, and they used conventional farming methods, which meant heavy use of chemicals and pesticides. But the Goodmans were convinced that organic farming was the way to go, and they didn't want chemicals in their land, in their food, or in their bodies. They began experimenting with new kinds of lettuce, such as baby greens, which were uncommon in salad fare back then.[22]

Since the couple had already been washing, bagging, and refrigerating some of the lettuce for their own meals, they wondered if they could possibly do the same thing with their produce for which they suddenly needed to find a buyer. "We were left with all this lettuce," Myra Goodman says. "We remembered how convenient our nightly bags of salad were and decided to try to make and sell these to local grocery and gourmet stores."[23] The stores weren't optimistic, but to their surprise, Earthbound Farm organic packaged salad mixes did sell, and the Goodmans had a whole new distribution channel and way of selling their produce.

As Samantha explains it, "One of the keys to this company's success is that Drew and Myra stuck to organic, even when everybody told them they couldn't do it." The Goodmans' commitment to organic products—and their flexibility about how to sell them—paid off handsomely in 1996 when they were approached by retailing giant Costco. Costco wanted to sell their packaged lettuce but did not want the packaging to say "organic" because at that time, organic produce was considered expensive and not of high quality. The Goodmans knew this was a great opportunity to grow their business, so they redesigned the packaging for the Costco lettuce.[24] Their entry as a Costco supplier helped give their brand, as well as organic foods in general, a huge boost.

The Goodmans stayed true to their organic values when they repackaged their lettuce for Costco, but they were willing to make changes to meet Costco's needs. The result was a win-win situation for both the retailer and for Earthbound Farm.

\*\*\*

We end this chapter with a short story highlighting Dancing Deer Baking Company of Boston and how happenstance propelled the company into the direct-to-consumer business.

When you're baking cookies and cakes for local cafes and restaurants and just trying to get your business established, thoughts of shipping your products all over the country may not be foremost in your mind. However, Trish Karter and the other cofounders of Dancing Deer discovered quickly that sudden publicity can be a real force in causing a business to either act and take advantage of the expansion opportunity at hand or do nothing and stay small and rooted where it is.

The situation was one right out of the movies, and it's only fitting that it was a man from Hollywood who propelled Dancing Deer into the spotlight. This food writer showed up in the bakery looking for directions. The products caught his attention—and obviously wowed his taste buds—and soon the bakery was being touted on national television as making the best cake in America. Dancing Deer decided to act on the amazing opportunity that had suddenly landed at its doorstep. Within twenty-four hours the bakery had a toll-free number up and running and found itself shipping cakes all over the country.[25]

Dancing Deer's decision to take advantage of this change in how they sold their product has paid off, and today the bakery continues to find new and profitable ways to build its business.

---

## COLLECTIVE WISDOM

• **Know your distributors.** If you sell your product through several distribution channels, understand the needs of each and how you can best serve those needs.

• **Place your product wisely.** Where your product is available may be critical to building your brand and supporting your core values. Develop strong relationships with distributors you feel match your mission.

• **Be passionate.** By promoting your product with enthusiasm, you become your business's number one cheerleader. Never overlook an opportunity to tell others, especially those connected to your distribution channel, how terrific your product is and why it should be available to purchase.

• **Determine your differentiation.** Be clear about why your product stands out in the marketplace and use this knowledge to your advantage in selling to your distributors. This approach is especially important if your product is one of many that buyers can choose from.

---

• **Keep it simple.** People are busy and appreciate ways to simplify their lives. If you make it easy for your customers to buy a quality product, chances are they'll keep buying it. And if you reward them for recommending your product to others, you expand your distribution with powerful word-of-mouth advertising.

• **Be flexible.** Change happens, and you will be presented with situations that can offer challenges as well as opportunities. Be bold when a problem surfaces and see how you can turn it into a new approach for increasing sales.

# 4

# Empowering your way to success

THE CREATIVE CHALLENGE: Finding a way to empower those connected to your business to build loyalty, enthusiasm, and a commitment to your values—and sales efforts

Employees are an integral part of your operation. How you treat them can make a difference in how they sell, show up for work, package and handle your product, and even treat customers. Dal LaMagna, founder of Tweezerman, made a decision from day one that he would not exploit his employees—"ever." In fact, Dal maintained a commitment to finding ways to empower his employees so they would be key beneficiaries of the company. One way he did this was to distribute stock to his employees in the form of an employee stock option plan. He felt that giving his employees ownership empowered them to be more responsible and engaged to help ensure the company's success, as well as their long-term benefits. When Dal sold the company in 2004, longtime Tweezerman employees who had received stock benefited handsomely—some gaining close to a million dollars.[1]

When it comes to selling a product or service, a sense of empowerment can be priceless. Empowered individuals radiate confidence, passion, and pride. If you are able to instill this attitude in those connected to your business, from employees to suppliers and distributors and even your customers, you will have a powerful advantage in not only increasing your sales but developing long-term and highly loyal relationships.

In this chapter we will look at some ways that businesses have managed to foster empowerment while taking their companies to new levels of success. For them, empowerment is all about good business practices that contribute to profitability.

Quite often, empowered individuals are the ones who take a leap of faith in the business world and try something new with the thought that it will boost sales or streamline how products get to customers. Or they rethink an old distribution method and retool it so the system is leaner and more beneficial to the company's bottom line. And sometimes an empowered businessperson decides to change direction altogether, even if this means that sales may temporarily slump while a new and better strategy is put in place.

In the following examples, you'll see how empowering others can help you fulfill your sales goals. This may mean immediate increased profits or a more visible presence in the marketplace (which can translate into future profits). Or it may mean you'll create a healthier, happier work environment that results in greater productivity. People who are empowered feel better about themselves. If they are employees, they may work harder or make a stronger commitment to your organization. If they are your customers, empowering them may result in larger sales or repeat sales, even when someone else offers a better price. And if they are members of your community, you have an opportunity to create synergistic relationships with them, which could result in an environment that helps you attract a more educated and enthusiastic work-force or win-win partnerships.

To empower means to give strength—in one's convictions, in one's self-confidence, in one's ability to make positive changes. There are many ways to empower those who are related to your business and its day-to-day activities as well as its overall success. Your choice as a business owner is to determine what empowerment means to your business and how it will translate into greater sales or more efficient distribution.

We've divided this chapter's lessons into Empowerment Strategies. Of course, the first person who must be empowered in your business is you. You must believe in your idea and your ability to make it work. However, by empowering others, you can improve your entire organization and your ability to make more sales.

## EMPOWERMENT STRATEGY NUMBER ONE: Educate your suppliers.

Starting at the source can be a powerful way to improve your bottom line as well as provide more profits for your suppliers. If your product originates from a culture not familiar with modern marketing practices, you will improve your ability to sell the product if you help your suppliers understand the value of high-quality raw materials and uniform standards. Training them on ways to improve their techniques and efficiency is important, and it may be beneficial to provide them with equipment or better (e.g., cleaner, more spacious, or more sanitary) working conditions so their productivity increases. Developing a flexible payment plan can help them procure materials and meet your order deadlines.

Education translates into empowerment when you show someone how to make a better product more efficiently. And if working conditions are improved, suppliers are more likely to receive more for their work and provide you with the product quantity you need to help you grow your business. This results in a powerful win-win situation.

Empowering your suppliers—no matter who they are or where they are located—often has long-term effects that can pay off handsomely. Investing in your suppliers' businesses may enable them to improve their day-to-day operations so they turn out a better product. Educating them on how to find higher-quality ingredients can also give you a more saleable product.

Here's an example of a company that created real power—for all concerned—and more sales by educating its suppliers.

## Watering the Seeds

Indigenous Designs Corporation has created highly beneficial relationships with the indigenous artisans who weave the company's articles of clothing. The company's garments are produced by family-owned enterprises or artisan-owned cooperatives primarily in Peru, Ecuador, and India. The company adheres strictly to Fair Trade and ecologically sustainable business practices and ensures that its suppliers also follow these practices with all raw material procurement and production related to the business. In addition, Indigenous Designs focuses on helping local artisans preserve their family and social infrastructure and culturally based skills.

The heart of Indigenous Designs' business is these family-run enterprises and cooperatives. The company has developed a finely tuned global production infrastructure within these communities, forming a network of over 260 artisan production groups around the globe. To help support these communities, Indigenous Designs pays two to three times the average wage for hand-knit apparel. This income has benefited indigenous artisans in remote communities all over the world.[2]

This emphasis on the family structure has guided the company in several ways and has enabled it to improve the lives of these artisans and their family members. An important point to remember is that by improving the lives of these people, Indigenous Designs is helping them to be more productive. Again, this creates a cycle of positive results: The artisans produce a higher-quality product that is more saleable and can be sold for a higher price. This gives them more profits and in turn helps Indigenous Designs grow as a business so it can continue to place orders.

Another way the company supports the artisans is by providing them with better equipment. In the past, before knitting garments for Indigenous Designs, these artisans had no way to assess their true market value and frequently exchanged their hand-knit products for food. The artisans also often used old bicycle spokes as knitting needles. Indigenous Designs has been able to provide them with appropriate needles at no cost. By teaching these people the value of their work and finished products, the company has been able to help them work more efficiently and obtain higher-quality yarns. In addition, the company offers free training and the opportunity to advance as a trainer.[3]

The company helps support the family unit through its payment system. Although the company does not interfere with the family infrastructure, it has been interested in paying—directly—the women who actually do the work. In many of these cultures, it is traditionally the men who collect the money earned within the family. Because Indigenous Designs uses NGOs to help distribute the women's earnings through the cooperatives that are formed, the women have become part of a collective group. As part of this group, the women receive support and guidance that help them in all aspects of their daily lives and as wage-earning artisans.

"There's a strong partnership with these women," says Scott Leonard, Indigenous Design's CEO and cofounder, "where they are congregating and putting their voices together. And that's really powerful."[4]

Indigenous Designs has found that if the women receive the money, they use it to make life better for their families. In this way, the women are "really watering the seeds of everything in the home," adds Scott. "And the idea is that, lo and behold, when you start to give money to these women in supporting the family unit, guess what the purchases tend to be about? They tend to be about things like good food, school supplies, things that really embrace the family unit."[5]

Scott has discovered that education—in a variety of ways—can empower entire communities. From providing flexible work hours to healthier work environments to instruction that helps the artisans set a fair price for each garment, Indigenous Designs is improving its suppliers' lives as it builds revenue for the company.[6]

# EMPOWERMENT STRATEGY NUMBER TWO: Seek input on how you make or market your product from your entire customer base.

Consider your target audience or customer. Now look a little deeper. For example, if you're selling an innovative software program to elementary schools that helps teachers manage their class schedules, students, and assignments, find a way to involve teachers in your product development and marketing. Even though they aren't the ones actually buying the software, they are the people *using* the software. And making them happy could be good for you when you approach the schools for future orders.

You can engage your customers in many ways as you go about strengthening your product line, service, or distribution methods. From research and development to outreach initiatives and strategic alliances, involving your customers can be educational and profitable for you and rewarding for them. This is especially true if your product serves a particular segment of the population. If you open your mind to a wide range of possibilities and *listen* to those who may have a need for your product (or a variation of it), you will find that innovation never stops—which is a big plus in increasing and maintaining strong sales.

Focus groups are common in the world of marketing, and you can create your own. Whether you're considering packaging, product design, color, name, or any of a host of other questions regarding your product and how it will be perceived in the marketplace, solicit feedback from individuals in your target group and beyond. People like to be asked their opinion, especially if they feel they're part of a special group or team that is responsible for helping to make important decisions. An advisory panel is a great way to get people on board, and it offers the opportunity to routinely add and replace participants over a span of time. Again, seek counsel from a wide range of individuals connected to your product or business.

Wild Planet Toys found out early in its development that some of its most valuable product allies were short on years but long on creativity. Here are some ways this innovative company has used this valuable segment of the population to help add new products to its line and boost sales.

## He Really Wants to Get Back to His Homework

Founded in 1993 by Daniel Grossman, San Francisco, California-based Wild Planet is all about toys. And who knows toys better than the people who play with them: kids. And that's exactly the people Daniel and Wild Planet are empowering with their innovative programs.

Getting children involved in the business as "inventors" and "advisers" happened very organically for the company. Although the company was committed from the start to providing community service, the idea of asking kids to help create toys evolved from a Wild Planet curriculum that involved working with kids on inventions. "One of the kids came up with this idea," explains Daniel. "And when we got back to the office, we sort of sat around and looked at it and said, 'Hey, you know, this is something! There might be something here.' So we mocked it up and made a model of it." They began to show the prototype to children, who loved it. On that basis, the company took the toy to market, and it was very successful.[7]

The product that materialized from the young boy's thinking was the Light Hand, and the inventor is still receiving royalties ten years later. This experience led to a collaboration with a boy who was nine when he started designing toys for Wild Planet. The boy's first toy was an underwater walkie-talkie called the Water Talkie, and he went on to invent a line of toys designed for the swimming pool. Three years later, at age twelve, his parents told Daniel that the boy would like to sell his "company" because he really wanted to get back to his homework. "That experience of working with this boy at that level and understanding his motivation and fulfilling his dream," adds Daniel, "in many ways was a huge impetus toward continuing to move in the direction of working with kids on that basis."[8]

The youthful ingenuity exhibited by these two boys helped Wild Planet develop its Kid Inventor Challenge and TOP (Toy Opinion Panel). The Kid Inventor Challenge invites elementary school children between the ages of six and twelve to invent their own toy. One hundred winners are selected each year to join a panel of special advisers—toy consultants—to the design team at Wild Planet for an entire year. After all, "Nothing motivates kids like a chance to have fun, be creative, and do something original—like inventing a toy."[9]

TOP is a program that invites parents and children to help Wild Planet design the toys of tomorrow. The company has created ways for families to participate whether they're in northern California or clear across the country. Those not in the San Francisco vicinity test "top secret" toy ideas by joining Wild Planet's Toy Advisory Panel. Throughout the year they receive e-mail invitations to participate in surveys or online discussion groups. Panel members have an opportunity to offer opinions on everything from new toy ideas to their taste in music. And children have the chance to win cool toys (with their parents' permission).

Those who live in northern California are encouraged to host a Toy Opinion Party at their school or home, for which they arrange for a group of five or six kids to get together. Wild Planet representatives then go to the location with toys to demonstrate to the group. The sessions are about an hour long, and every child receives a toy. Adults are also rewarded for acting as hosts. In addition, Wild Planet invites schools and community organizations to participate in the TOP program, with hosts qualifying to receive a donation for their class or program.[10]

For Daniel, the heart of what Wild Planet does is really wrapped up in the company's approach to creating popular toys and what that means to kids. "Parents really love this [invention] program," says Daniel. "They intuitively understand and they see in their kids' reactions and their faces that it's such a huge boost in self-esteem to them when they get respected by adults for something that they do."[11]

As Daniel Grossman and Wild Planet are demonstrating, empowering children is one way to make a difference in the world. Children are learning at an early age that their opinions count and that they are free to be as "outside the box" as they like when it comes to creating a toy. They're also learning the power of focusing on an idea and believing in themselves as they develop those ideas.

We add one other thought to this lesson: will these children think of Wild Planet when they're buying toys for themselves (and their children) in the future, and will their parents and teachers think of Wild Planet today? We believe the answer is a definite yes.

# EMPOWERMENT STRATEGY NUMBER THREE: Instill passion—and

# loyalty—in your employees through education.

Mentoring is nothing new in the business world. But it may be the last thing you think about when you're putting together a business plan and building strategies for selling your product or service. However, most businesses, especially if they experience rapid growth, are always looking for capable and dedicated employees.

An internship or mentoring program can be highly beneficial to a business. Here are a few ideas: Create a program that allows college students to gain experience by working at your company. Develop a partnership with a local university so the students earn credits for their work with you. Organize outreach programs that promote an exchange of ideas with individuals in the community who share some of your business goals.

As you are planning your mentoring program, think about what you wish you could have learned at a younger age. If your interns are high school or college students, consider the practical aspects of your business that will benefit them when they are looking for a job after graduation or possibly running their own businesses. These may include how to write a business plan, how to read a profit and loss statement, or even something as routine as how to pack and ship breakable merchandise. And learning at an early age how to treat customers with courtesy and respect is a skill that will stay with a person for a lifetime.

In addition to teaching skills to your interns, take time to listen to their ideas and seek their feedback about your operation. The more you can engage these business leaders of tomorrow in your operation, the more passion you will foster within them. And increased profits often begin with embracing the enthusiasm and creativity of those around you.

Hidden Beach Recordings is dedicated to giving artists the opportunity to present their music as they truly want it to be heard—and felt. But as the next example shows, the company has also discovered the dynamic potential that exists within those who are passionate about working in the entertainment industry and are willing to learn on the job.

## *Staying True to Your Soul*

Hidden Beach Recordings is using the power and gift of music to empower individuals in diverse, innovative ways. Steve McKeever, the founder of Hidden Beach, based in Santa Monica, California, acts as the company's chief executive and oversees all of Hidden Beach's day-to-day operations. The company's mission is to present passion-filled artists and encourage them to stay true to their soul and emotional center. A former executive with Polygram Records and Motown Records, Steve is well versed in introducing new recording artists to the public and turning such talent into successful endeavors for the companies that represent them. His company is the culmination of his professional vision of creating a uniquely independent music outlet committed to setting new artistic and business standards for the entertainment community. In short, he wants to build one of the new industry "brands" consumers can trust and embrace.[12]

In addition to creating a safe artistic haven for his artists, Steve has initiated a program that helps young people become involved in all aspects of the music business. Hidden Beach Recordings' College Internship Program is an international effort that provides college students with hands-on music-business experience. The company has had as many as 540 students in the program, and Steve hopes to up that number to 2,000 and make it a model for the entertainment industry.

Steve has long dreamed of fostering a program of this kind. He calls it the "heartbeat of what we do here" and considers it to be symbiotic with the company. He started the College Internship Program because he wanted to create something that he wished had been available when he was young. The idea for it began to germinate fifteen years ago when Steve was an executive at Motown. But the legal concerns that tend to percolate in big business derailed the program, and Steve was forced to abandon the idea.[13]

When Steve formed Hidden Beach Recordings, he resurrected the idea and discussed it with a student helping him with the business. The young man presented the program to his class at the university he attended, and Steve instantly received thirty-five enthusiastic e-mails from the students. "They were so desperate to learn about the business of how things really worked and get hands-on experience in a place where it was really tough, that they would do anything," says Steve. Realizing he needed more help to manage a program like this, Steve spent over a year brainstorming and fine-tuning the details of his College Internship Program. He focused on the skills and knowledge he wished he could have gained as a young man and how he could empower college students eager to learn about the recording industry.

The application requirements for Hidden Beach Recordings' internship program are simple: the students have to be enrolled in a college class, must write two essays, and must provide two letters of recommendation. Steve is looking for students who have a real passion for the business and who really want to learn, as opposed to those with a stellar grade point average. "Anybody who's passionate, for the most part, comes in the door," he says. "What they've learned is 'My ideas are extraordinarily valuable.' And most importantly, they get empowered to learn that if they follow their passions about what they love and do what they love, then it will reward them ten times over." Hidden Beach's interns do real work, working directly with the artists the company represents. In the case of one of the label's superstars, Jill Scott, interns were involved in every phase of the marketing campaign that helped propel her from unknown to Grammy Award winner.[14]

Steve is especially proud that he's been able to hire interns to fill positions at Hidden Beach—even the head of the internship program was once an intern. He likens the program to a baseball farm team, where the outstanding players are recruited to play for the majors. In addition, the company holds conventions around the country where the interns are invited to gather and talk with members of the home office. The interns have also created a little viral network of their own, a kind of fraternity or sorority, so if they need help or a contact in a city they're visiting, they can call on one another for support.

For Steve, his College Internship Program is an idea that took years to come to maturity but is finally paying off with handsome dividends. "I was this kid who would have done anything, anytime, anywhere, just to be in the industry," he adds. "Sweep floors, whatever it took to get in because that was my passion." And now, that kid opens new opportunities in the lives of the students who intern for his company. "If you're in the program, you're completely empowered to go for it."[15]

# EMPOWERMENT STRATEGY NUMBER FOUR: Use financial incentives coupled with a strong sense of belonging to build loyalty and confidence among your sales force.

Let's face it: when you're the one paying the bills, coming up with the marketing plans, and struggling to keep products in the warehouse and shipping them on time, it can be tempting to squeeze out every possible percentage of gross income. When you have a large sales force, as direct-selling companies have, you might be tempted to keep the commissions as lean as possible. However, if you reward your sales force as much as you can, the long-term gains may outweigh the short-term pains.

Later in the book, we'll discuss the benefits of recognizing and celebrating the accomplishments of your sales force. But another factor can build a strong sense of unity among the members of a sales team.

It is the notion of empowerment shared by a group of like-minded individuals. Although individual achievements play a significant role in meeting sales goals for any organization, the concept of creating *communities* of support can be a powerful way to foster a ripple effect of success.

This concept is especially applicable to direct-selling companies since commissions and bonuses are often paid to sales representatives based on the performance of their entire group. However, in many businesses, sales representatives are paid bonuses if the organization as a whole meets its sales goals. By promoting an atmosphere of team building, you can help each salesperson be more successful, which leads to more success for your business overall.

In the case of Warm Spirit, which has continually paid between 10 and 15 percent more in commissions to its consultants than the industry average, one of the most powerful aspects of its organizational support system is the strong sense of community Nadine has fostered since the company's creation. This goes back to her belief that black women need opportunities to feel good about themselves and to understand that it is possible to achieve new goals and make dreams come true. The philosophy appears to be paying off as the company continues to realize steady growth in both revenue and the number of new consultants.

# *The Beauty of Community*

Nadine's mission of empowering African American women is paramount to building not only a strong company but also more confident and successful consultants. As Warm Spirit consultants have embraced the company's business opportunity and the benefits of its products, they have reached out to other people and created organizations of their own, which have become individual communities of empowerment. Here, women and men are able to coach one another and help each other reach their goals and also feel comfortable sharing their spirituality and stories—the challenges as well as the successes.

To Nadine, a community is a place where people are likeminded and supportive and share common goals. It's where people are able to exist together in a respectful way. Nadine feels Warm Spirit has created communities of empowered entrepreneurs who are business savvy and upwardly mobile and understand the value of money. For her, this sense of community and the network of people that has been created around the country is priceless.

Fostering communities where people feel safe and comfortable yet challenged to grow is a large part of what Nadine stresses when she talks about Warm Spirit. She wants the consultants to be able to tell their stories and have people bear witness to their transformation as more empowered individuals. And once this transformation takes place, they can begin to experience a real sense of accomplishment and self-esteem.

As the self-described "mother hen" of this community, Nadine also feels protective. She is approached routinely by people who want to reach this community of consultants—people from other companies who want access to these individuals so they can sell them their merchandise or services. She must carefully weigh the opportunities that are presented and choose the relationships she feels are most beneficial to the consultants and compatible with the company's values. Her first concern in considering these opportunities is whether they really add to the quality of the consultants' lives. In evaluating each one, she asks, Will it help them build a more successful business? Will it improve their lives spiritually, physically, or financially? Or is it simply an item that consultants are asked to invest in but really has no long-lasting value?

By continuing to build this sense of community throughout the Warm Spirit operation, she feels the company's growth will increase as more and more people work together to fulfill their like-minded aspirations.

# EMPOWERMENT STRATEGY NUMBER FIVE: Determine your standards early in the game and base your business relationships on these standards.

The beauty of figuring out your value system when you start building your business is that it keeps you on course. Since people are an integral part of any business, it's important that you are clear about how you want to treat people connected to your business and why you believe that will translate into more sales and increased revenue growth.

This attitude carries over into whom you hire (e.g., people from your local community), how you involve them in the success of your business, and even how much you pay them and the benefits you make available to them. Our opening example highlights a profit-sharing plan developed by Dal LaMagna that ended up paying huge dividends to many of his employees. His determination—from the start of creating his company—to operate with what he calls "responsible capitalism" enabled him to take the steps that would build this program.

Other people connected to your business can also help you build sales and navigate challenges that erupt during the course of running your business. If you treat your suppliers with integrity, they may be more understanding if you need extra time to pay them or want to adjust your ordering process. If they trust you and your ability to sell unique products, they may be willing to experiment with formulas and invest in new ingredients to develop a new product for you.

Your customers also deserve respect and a sense of empowerment in their own right. The values you have set as a company and as a business owner extend to the product or service you are selling. In other words, if you attach your values to your product by offering a money-back guarantee, free repair or replacement, a guaranteed response time for problems, or 24/7 customer service, you strengthen your customers' loyalty to your brand, which can result in repeat sales, even when a less expensive, similar product is available.

Your investors are a critical component of your operation. You can empower them by making sure your values are aligned with theirs as you develop each aspect of your business. You have far more strength as a team than as individuals who may each have his or her own agenda for how the business should operate or grow. If your investors support your vision and your values as a company, they will be more willing to support you when it comes time to expand or try a new business venture.

You can also empower your community. By making the organizations and people within your community part of your day-to-day business operation, you create long-lasting relationships that can support you in a variety of ways: by providing you with a higher-caliber workforce, by giving you strategic alliances for special promotions, by helping you generate publicity about your business, and by fostering a positive attitude that helps promote a strong customer base.

We end this chapter with an example from an entrepreneur who built his company on a strong platform of values. At the end of the day, everyone benefited, proving that using your values as a source of empowerment can yield impressive results.

## *Tell Him I Don't Want to Talk to Him!*

Dal LaMagna, who created the Tweezerman brand of personal grooming tools, knew from the very start of his burgeoning enterprise that he wanted to run his business differently. He had a beat in his head that resonated in his heart, and he always marched to that rhythm as he took Tweezerman, based in Port Washington, New York, from a business that earned him $100 a day in sales to over $30 million when he sold the company in December 2004. He had specific ideas about how he would treat his employees, his customers, his shareholders, his suppliers, and his community.

For Dal, business growth was coupled with doing right by those who were working for him and providing the day-to-day support that enabled him to promote the brand. Although he was a 1970 Harvard Business School graduate, he knew what it was like not to have income. And perhaps this lack of money proved to be fortuitous in helping him establish his own guidelines for how he would operate his business. In 1980, when he first came up with the idea for his needle-nose tweezers, he attended his tenth-year reunion at the business school. His less-than-impressive annual earnings of $1,280 once caused a classmate to point out that he "had caused the class earnings average to drop by $80."[16]

In business school he learned early on that many in the business world considered the bottom line and profits to be the governing force for a company. And that wasn't how this entrepreneur wanted to do business. The notion that the shareholder is king did not sit well with Dal. "I just could not, in my heart, follow that advice," he says. He had his own agenda items for creating a successful company, and empowering his employees was one of them.[17]

Dal knew that many of his classmates had gone on to work on Wall Street, where it was common for employees to work eighty to ninety hours a week on salary. They worked nights and weekends and never received any overtime pay. He decided to pay his employees an hourly wage so they always got paid for the hours they worked. "I always kept ahead of the curve. I strived to pay what I considered to be enough for a person to live." He also set up a health plan as soon as he had enough employees.[18]

Offering flextime was also important to Dal. He initially had a lot of women working for him, and when a pregnant employee was close to her due date, he told her to go home, have the baby, and come back in three months because he would hold the job for her. To Dal, this was simply a matter of empowering his employees. "I consciously elevated the employee to the same status of beneficiary as the customer and the shareholder. So I had these three critical share-holders."[19]

Another interesting aspect of Dal's respect for his employees is evidenced by his decision to sell the company when he did. Active in politics, he began to worry that his involvement would cause political ene-mies to come after him and drive away major cus-tomers, which could decimate the stock value. And at this point, Tweezerman was growing 10 percent a year. "I wanted, at the end of the day," he says, "to protect not only my own wealth which was all in the company, but also the employees. Because the employees had a big stake by this point. I didn't think it was fair to my employees to take them on this political ride."[20]

When eight potential buyers appeared, Dal decided to sell. But first, in true Dal style, he had some rules—rules that held firm to the values he had established from day one. One, no layoffs could be conducted by the acquiring company; two, Tweezerman wasn't to be moved to another location; three, the acquiring company would continue to practice responsible capitalism; and four, the acquiring company would pay "an obscene amount of money." The acquiring company, the Zwilling J.A. Henckels Company (a German, family-owned business famous for its knives), agreed to Dal's terms, and today Tweezerman continues to grow and the brand remains strong.[21]

Another way Dal fueled the growth of his company was by empowering his suppliers. He did this by always treating them with respect and being honest with them in the early days when money was tight. And his attitude paid off. "I was very careful not to exploit my suppliers. I was loyal to them." This loyalty was expressed in several ways: by giving suppliers a chance to meet a lower bid quoted by a competitor; by keeping in touch with vendors when, in the early days, he knew he'd be late paying them; and by paying interest when his payment was late. "They never held back," he says. "They trusted me, and it just became a very smart strategy to be responsible to your vendors."[22]

Honesty was also important to Dal. He paid for personal photocopies made at the office, and he created a corporate culture of not lying, which put him in the spotlight more than once, especially when he was faced with a phone call he did not want to take. "My assistant would try to catch me in a lie, so she'd come in my room. She'd say, 'Oh, I've got somebody on the phone. What do you want me to tell him? Should I tell him you're not in?' I said, 'No! Tell  him I don't want to talk to him!'"[23]

And how did Dal empower his customers? By offering a lifetime guarantee on his tweezers. At $20, they weren't the cheapest tweezers available. But by selling "tweezing" as opposed to tweezers, Dal fostered loyalty and peace of mind among his customers. Tweezerman would repair, sharpen, or replace damaged tweezers free of charge and also pay all shipping costs. An added benefit of this policy was that the damaged tweezers did not end up in a landfill, which added sustainability to the mix. Dal could also return each repaired or replaced tweezer with information about other products. He believes this service was the biggest driver for new customers.

With his responsible treatment of his employees, suppliers, and customers, Dal was able to maintain the growth of the company, which in turn made shareholders happy—a definite source of empowerment for them. And finally, the community was another factor in Dal's game plan when it came to operating under the "responsible capitalism" banner. "The community, for me, was my neighborhood," he says. "We always strived to hire from the neighborhood. We usually put up a sign in front of the building. But also, we would give back." The company budgeted 5 percent of its profits to the community.[24]

Dal firmly believes that Tweezerman's success is directly related to the empowering and doing-well-by-doing-good policies he built into the company right from the beginning. "I think that practicing responsible capitalism, for Tweezerman at least, probably increased its value, at the end of the day, by 50 percent."[25]

---

## COLLECTIVE WISDOM

• **Enhance your suppliers' ability to perform.** This may mean finding ways to educate them about the value of using high-quality ingredients, improving their working conditions, investing in equipment, or providing them with knowledge about good business practices.

• **Solicit advice from beyond your primary customer target.** Consider everyone connected to your business, and ask yourself how others might use your product or service. Think about all the ways your product benefits people, even if they aren't the end consumer, and find out how they think the product could be improved.

• **Invest in a mentoring program.** Speak to schools and local organizations whose members may be interested in what you do—and how you're doing it. Providing on-the-job training for those who are passionate about your business or industry is an excellent way to find and keep competent employees.

• **Determine your business's "community."** Make a list of those who have a vested interest in your business. This could include employees, investors, suppliers, and even customers. Then come up with strategic ways to connect them so a sense of community, in the form of shared goals, is created.

• **Use your values to empower others.** Determine early in your planning how you will use your values to empower everyone connected to your business. Be clear about and committed to each of these empowerment strategies and how they will build strong relationships.

# 5

# Educating your partners

## THE CREATIVE CHALLENGE: Using education to build awareness of your product and enthusiasm for how it can benefit customers' lives

Earth Creations is an Alabama company with strong ties to the earth. That's because its organic cotton and hemp clothing is dyed with clay. Everything husband and wife owners Martin Ledvina and Joy Maples do is focused on their tagline: "The environmental answer for apparel." And educating those in their distribution channel is a big part of this effort. Joy wanted to attract retailers to Earth Creations' booth at trade shows, so she created little campaigns. About three or four months prior to the show date, she sends marketing materials to those attending the show. For one campaign, she used the theme "You reap what you sow" and put a packet of organic seeds in the marketing package. Joy used this device to illustrate the idea of sowing seeds in your store and growing your business by educating your customers. The campaign was successful, catching the attention of retailers and giving Joy appointments with 80 percent of her target customers.[1]

For most businesses, the driving force behind their success is their product. Make an inferior product, a product that is not in step with current trends, or one that people don't want to buy again, and you have a recipe for disaster. And if you have a high-quality product that is in demand, you must make sure the product meets your standards—and your customers' standards—each and every time it is sold. The same philosophy holds true for the way you convey your message (your mission, your commitment to your customers, your brand positioning) and the way your sales force presents the product benefits and your company.

Education can play a pivotal role in promoting your business and its product. Your education efforts should be aimed at your employees (for their own personal benefit as well as for your business's benefit), your customers, and the public as a whole.

In this chapter we'll examine companies that have created a wide variety of educational tools and services and implemented them into their daily operations to increase sales and build stronger distribution networks. Done well, education can help you build a business that matches both your socially responsible goals and your revenue target—without expensive advertising campaigns.

The following Support Strategies are designed to help you educate those connected to your business, which is often a vital step in helping people understand and embrace the value of your product and mission.

# SUPPORT STRATEGY NUMBER ONE: Educate the public about your product and mission and what differentiates them in the marketplace.

To put it simply, educated customers are often better customers. This is not a new concept in the business world, and successful businesses have been practicing it for years. What is important to remember, though, is that as a socially responsible company, you may be selling a product or service that is new to the public (in its design, ingredients, manufacture, or benefits) and may be priced higher than similar brands in the industry. For example, Honest Tea products sell for about 20 cents more than rival products. If company cofounder Seth Goldman never talked about his efforts to make the brand organic or to make every facet of Honest Tea's operation socially responsible, customers would not know and certainly would not understand why his product is more expensive and, most importantly, why it is worth buying.

You can use education in many ways to enhance who you are and what you're selling. Your business may lend itself to a true educational experience that you can market within your community. This may include developing a program for schools or other youth organizations in your area that educates children about your industry or your particular socially responsible mission. For example, if your mission is about respecting the environment, you could put together an environmental fair for local schools, sponsor an "improve the environment" contest, or organize and facilitate a recycling program involving school children.

You may want to conduct tours of your facility, during which you can educate those attending about your cause and how your product supports it. Special events that involve the community can be an excellent way to promote your mission and brand, and special offers that sell your product and promote your mission can be valuable ways to couple your sales with overall public awareness.

Your Web site is also a powerful tool. Create one that is interesting and interactive and that encourages people to explore. Then promote it and use it. You can put special offers on your site, promote new products, post press releases and news stories, and highlight customers, suppliers, and employees. If your product is food related, you may want to post recipes, hold a recipe contest, or invite people to write in with questions about your product or foods in general. Your Web site is also the perfect place to provide background information about ingredients that go into your products or detailed material about your industry. Once you have a great site established, promote it on all of your materials. Today a Web site address is as important as a phone number.

In planning how you can educate the public about your business, think about all of the ways your product touches people. As you meet the public, find out what people might like to know about your product or your industry. Consider ways you can educate them as you help them in some way. For example, holding an environmental essay contest for local schools in which the winners' essays are published in a local newspaper can generate publicity for you, raise overall awareness about environmental issues, and benefit the winners.

And finally, make use of your own driving passion and expertise about your business. For example, consider writing a book or crafting articles for magazines or newspapers, investigate becoming a guest on a local television or radio program, or talk to colleges and community educational programs about becoming a guest lecturer, seminar leader, or regular instructor.

## Championing the Environment Builds Sales

One company that uses education and an assortment of outreach programs to communicate with the public—and build strong relationships with its customers—is Mountain Equipment Co-op (MEC), based in Vancouver, British Columbia. MEC is Canada's largest supplier of quality outdoor equipment, with 2.3 million members in 192 countries. MEC has eleven stores across Canada as well as a comprehensive Web store and phone/mail order service. As a co-op, MEC sets its prices to cover costs, not maximize profits. Members are also part owners who vote for the company's board of directors. According to the Web site, people, not capital, control MEC.[2]

MEC does not engage in traditional retail marketing tactics in terms of flyers and sales, and because maximizing profits isn't the objective, prices are kept as low as possible. The company does little advertising in magazines and rarely runs ads in newspapers. According to Peter ter Weeme, chief communications and marketing officer, the vast majority of MEC's members come to the company by word of mouth and through the reputation of the organization. In fact, one in ten Canadian adults belongs to the co-op, giving the company a substantial market share in the outdoor equipment industry.

"All of the decisions we make as a business are filtered through the lens of social-environmental responsibility," says Peter. "Our purpose as an organization is to help people achieve the benefits of what we call 'self-propelled outdoor recreation.' And that means you have to do the work. In other words, cross-country skiing versus downhill skiing." According to Peter, MEC's business is about getting people outdoors and into nature. The company is committed to acting as a champion of the environment—to educate people about the environment and how to use it. "If we aren't good stewards of the environment and ensure there are places that people can access in order to practice those activities," adds Peter, "we're going to have a real hard time maintaining our relevance."[3]

To this end, the co-op aligns itself with organizations in Canada that support its mission, including the Canadian Parks and Wilderness Society, the Alpine Club of Canada, Leave No Trace Behind, and the Canadian Recreational Canoe Association. In addition, MEC has created a "Clubs and Groups Strategy" designed to create relationships between the co-op and people who engage in activities for which MEC sells equipment. This philosophy plays a role in reminding people that they can go to MEC for their outdoor recreation equipment.

Because MEC doesn't do a lot of advertising, its emphasis on partnering with organizations that further its mission, educating the public about conservation, and acting as a socially responsible company in general has paid off enormously in Peter's eyes, even though MEC cannot determine to what degree people are increasing their frequency of purchase or their size of transaction. However, MEC did some research on its members to look at how much of their connection to the company was based on its products and services and how much was based on the values of the organization. Peter says the researchers discovered that roughly 70 percent of MEC's members are very strongly attracted to the co-op on the basis of its values.

In addition, the co-op's actions result in an incredible amount of media attention, which Peter equates to over a million dollars a year in free publicity. And of course, publicity helps identify who you are in the business world. And finally, the co-op's continual education to the public about its social-environmental values has helped pave the way for MEC's launch into new markets. Says Peter, "We get people lining up from government levels as well as other business community leaders saying, 'How can we help you? How can we smooth the path? You're a great company; we want you in our town. We want you in our city.' That's a very different equation than Wal-Mart, for example, which has been beaten out of communities."[4]

All of this amounts to loyal customers who are educated not only by the co-op's ongoing social-environmental  efforts but also by MEC staff members, who are noncommissioned and trained to provide customers with the information and equipment they need. "There's a level of respect that takes place between the member and the employee serving them, and that has been an important part of our secret of success, and people respond very well to that," Peter adds.[5]

# SUPPORT STRATEGY NUMBER TWO: Be clear about what your brand represents and how you want to present it.

For business, the brand can be everything. High-priced advertising agencies spend millions of their clients' dollars ensuring that their brands are not only visible but clearly defined and uniform. Educating the public with strong brand messages is integral to many advertising campaigns. Chances are you won't have the dollars to spend on expensive advertising, but you can delineate your brand and make sure it is always presented so customers know *who you are* and *what they are buying* each and every time they make a purchase—and that can translate into continued and repeat sales.

Making sure your values are strongly connected to your brand is also an important part of the education process. MEC provides a good example of this concept. According to Peter, the MEC brand is based on four pillars: offering quality gear at the lowest, most reasonable price; carefully training its employees to help co-op members make the right decisions about the gear they need; focusing the co-op's attention on its social-environmental beliefs; and creating a sense of belonging in that each member is part owner of the co-op and also belongs to a greater community of outdoor recreation enthusiasts. Together, these pillars have built a strong brand and have turned MEC into a company with projected 2006 earnings of about US$180 million.[6]

According to Scott Mayhew, CEO of the image-branding design firm Corsair Studio, based in New York City, "The care in the way you build a brand really needs to be conscious—at the ownership level. And if not, it sort of falls apart. Or it gets more difficult." Scott believes this is especially critical for startup companies. For new businesses working with design firms, like his, a collaborative effort between the visionaries of the company and those helping to shape the brand is important. He feels incremental growth (versus large, fast growth) helps new companies get established, especially if they're aware of their audiences and strategies. Then as momentum builds, everything will start to click.[7]

Protecting your brand by duplicating it in the same fashion each time it is used and educating the public about your brand are critical factors in building awareness of your product. For example, if you allow other people with whom you are associated (such as partners in a special event) to use the brand on products that you have not created and do not match your quality standards, you run the risk of tainting your brand with inferior merchandise.

A good example of a company that retained its brand's integrity as the business expanded with new products and distribution channels is Tweezerman.

## *The Tweezerman Is Here!*

Dal LaMagna's journey to success got a unique, albeit *painful,* start over twenty-five years ago in California after a zesty encounter with a female friend on a wood sundeck. The episode left him with thirty-two redwood splinters in his rear, and he quickly discovered that he didn't have the right implement to remove them—he needed a combination tweezer and needle. So he put on his pants and set out to buy one. But none existed, so the splinter removal process was extremely slow (and painful). Fast forward to New York City a few months later where Dal was working at an electronics company. The instrument used to pick up capacitors and diodes was exactly what he had wanted. "I went, 'Whoa! Where'd you get those things?' Because, I'd just been so frustrated. You get an idea, and then you go try to find the product, and it's just impossible."[8]

Dal started buying the needle-nose tweezers from the European supplier, named them "splinter tweezers," and began calling on lumberyards and hardware stores. The store buyers doubted that the tweezers would sell, but they agreed to display them. And to their surprise, the product sold. When a friend who owned a beauty salon commented that she could use precision tweezers for shaping eyebrows, Dal found a jeweler's model that was pointed but not sharp, called them "precision eyebrow tweezers," and soon had beauty salons clamoring for his tweezers.

Throughout the growth of Tweezerman, Dal kept adding personal grooming tools as he found new customers and needs. But the one element he never fiddled with was the integrity of his brand, and this is the important lesson Dal's experience provides. "One of the rules I had was I would never split the brand. In other words, Tweezerman is Tweezerman," he explains. "Everyone kept saying, 'You have to use a different name when you're selling in the drugstores because the professional market's not going to tolerate the product being available in Walgreens.'" Dal solved this problem by creating variations of the name. For example, he had the Tweezerman Professional, Tweezerman Spa, and Tweezerman Limited lines. Each time he developed a new product line, he kept the Tweezerman name so he could continue to build the brand. Even when cosmetic giant Clinique came to Dal for a tweezer it could market, he held firm to this brand dedication. "On the Clinique tweezer, we said, 'Our name has to be on the tweezer beside theirs so we could focus on the name Tweezerman and stick with the brand.'"[9]

A final comment regarding the name Tweezerman. Dal was repeatedly told he should come up with a name denoting precision and quality—perhaps something Swiss sounding. He toyed with such ideas and even started out by putting his own name on his products. But the day he walked into a beauty salon and one of his previous buyers yelled, "The Tweezerman is here!" he knew he had found the perfect name. Even though some people felt he was making a terrible mistake, he stuck to it—to huge sales success. "I tell you," he adds, "I couldn't have come up with a better name. It was just too perfect."[10]

Remember that your brand is *you*—your product, your business, your integrity. As Dal discovered, branding his grooming products and never compromising the brand helped him increase sales and build customer loyalty. Many other companies have built extremely profitable businesses on their brands as well. Their brands tell consumers what to look for, what they are, and what they stand for.

## SUPPORT STRATEGY NUMBER THREE: Educate your employees so they can knowledgeably and enthusiastically share your mission and product benefits.

We've all encountered sales staff who sound less than enthused about the products they're selling. As we pointed out, one of MEC's strategies is to train its employees thoroughly about the company's products so they can help customers buy exactly what they need. This helps the co-op's members feel safe about shopping at MEC, knowing they won't be confronted with bait-and-switch tactics or be sold an item that doesn't fit their requirements.

Another way to educate your employees is by giving them more information about your mission and your industry and why you feel your mission is important to building a successful business. If your employees buy into your goals and actions as a company, they are far more likely to pass along your enthusiasm and knowledge to others they encounter—from regular customers to members of the general public who may *become* customers. And this translates into more effective sales.

You must first determine what makes your product unique and consider how you can train your employees so they can best explain this to your customers. Your unique selling proposition may involve the ingredients you use (or don't use, if you exclude harmful items that your competitors may include in similar products), the manufacturing process, and even alliances you may rely on in producing or distributing your products (such as Indigenous Designs' partnerships with NGOs and artisans). Educating your employees effectively is especially critical if your product has a higher price tag than some competitors' products.

In the following example you'll learn how one company makes educating its employees a critical component of its sales strategies.

## *Education Builds Brand Loyalty*

According to Dave Knutson, minister of human resources and sustainability at Chaco, Inc., based in Paonia, Colorado, a businessperson can choose from many different business models. "You can be a commodity and try to compete on price, or you can create value," he says. For the leaders at Chaco, creating value from the beginning and in the cus-tomer's mind that their product is worth a premium allows them to pay their employees decently and treat the planet well.[11]

By educating your customers, you are giving them valuable information to help them wade through a sea of products and make a decision that is based on quality, integrity, and values instead of price alone. Chaco does very little traditional advertising, but it thoroughly educates its customers by training its employees about the popular sandals. This philos-ophy results in powerful word-of-mouth "advertising" that has helped the company go from sales out of the founder's pickup to over $15 million in annual sales today.

The company began in 1989 when founder Mark Paigen decided he could make better river-rafting footwear than the tennis shoes and Velcro sandals that were then on the market. When he began look-ing for stores that would sell his brand, Mark focused on specialty stores and made sure their staff mem-bers knew what made a Chaco sandal different—and worth the price. Chaco has remained loyal to these stores, a strategy Dave feels has gone a long way toward building sales. But even outside the stores that carried Mark's brand, the sandals were gaining fans among river-rafting guides, which prompted rafters on their trips to ask where they could get them.

According to Dave, the sandals' high price was quickly offset by satisfied Chaco wearers, including salespeople in the specialty stores. "A customer might comment, 'Boy, these are awfully expensive! They look pretty simple.' The salesman will say, 'Well, we don't want you to put those on your feet because you'll have to buy them because, essentially, they feel so good on your feet. For the typical foot, it does great for motion control and cushioning, and just the whole feel of walking in a Chaco is huge."[12]

According to Dave, a Chaco sandal should fit a certain way. "You know, you don't just order off the Internet and throw it on your foot. We want people to understand how to adjust the straps and how close their toe should be to the front of the shoe, whether they need a wide or a narrow, and other things that may affect the proper fit." In addition, Chaco wants people to understand that they are buying durability along with fit and comfort—the sandals tend to last two or three times longer than other sandals.[13]

Dave believes that this attention to quality design and education about the sandal, as well as the company's loyalty to the specialty stores, has been instrumental in driving sales throughout Chaco's seventeen-year history.[14]

## SUPPORT STRATEGY NUMBER FOUR: Educate your distributors so they can better educate your end customer and increase sales.

Getting your product into stores is only part of the process of generating sales. Your product must then be purchased—again and again by the retailers' customers—for you to be successful. One way to help promote sales in stores is by educating the retailers that are purchasing from you. This requires giving them information about your product and what differentiates it in the marketplace, providing display materials so they can highlight your product, and offering price breaks for ordering in bulk or for a special promotion.

As you consider ways to promote your product to your distribution channel, think about how you connect its unique design, manufacture, or usage features into marketing materials and messages that consistently tell your product's story. You want your distributors to be familiar with your brand and your product and, hopefully, become excited about what it offers them as retailers. If those in your distribution channel feel really good about the product you're giving them to sell, and if you give them materials to help them display it, they will do a much better job of placing it in their stores to attract customers' attention.

# The Dirt on Educating Your Distribution Channel

Joy Maples and her husband always intended to sell wholesale. And they try hard to support the retailers through their educational and marketing materials. For example, for Earth Day they choose a few organic T-shirts with messages relevant to the day and make them available as a package, offering a discount for the purchase of a certain quantity. They also supply the retailers with a press release designed so they can fill in the blanks and send it to their local media outlets. In addition, Joy sends them point-of-purchase information to be placed on clothing racks that promotes the environment and how Earth Creations clothing is made, from the field to the end consumer, and why it is a quality item.

The press kits the company produces and distributes to the media also drive home the sustainability message. Each kit comes with a little plastic bag of dirt and includes samples of the company's garment tags, which describe some aspect of the fabric or the production process.

In the opening example we showed you how Joy created a campaign to entice retailers to visit Earth Creations' booth at trade shows. She focuses on her product's connection to the earth with each of these promotions, which helps underscore the company's mission to be environmentally responsible and the reason that Earth Creations clothing is worth buying to retailers and then promoting in their stores.[15]

***

Making a difference is really what education is all about. You've read about many ways and reasons to use education in developing strong sales and effective distribution. What is important is to think about what you can do and how you can carry out your education policies so they make a difference to your sales goals and overall revenue.

---

## COLLECTIVE WISDOM

• **Educate the public.** While focusing on customers is critical to building strong sales, you must also educate the public as a whole about your business and your product. Positive public awareness creates new customers. In everything you do, use your packaging, promote your industry, and take steps to highlight why your product is worth buying.

• **Maintain the integrity of your brand.** If you've done a good job of creating a name or slogan that identifies you in the marketplace, be sure to protect it. This means not compromising your brand by attaching it to inferior products or allowing outsiders to use it on their merchandise. If you develop new products, retain your brand identity.

• **Train your employees.** To sell your product effectively, your employees must understand your product and what makes it unique, they must understand your industry, they must embrace your mission, and they must be able to relay all of this information to your customers with passion and a shared sense of purpose.

• **Support your distributors.** Your distributors—those who are selling your product to the end customer—must also understand your product and your mission. If you can create strong allies among these individuals by providing them with materials that will help them sell your product, you'll enhance their ability to be successful—which will translate into more success for you.

# 6

# Creating valuable strategic alliances

## THE CREATIVE CHALLENGE: Aligning yourself with like-minded organizations so everyone benefits

As Myra and Drew Goodman's Earthbound Farm grew and began acquiring customers all over the country , the couple found themselves facing a challenge: how to grow all the food their burgeoning enterprise was demanding. Not only did they need more acreage, they needed to know how to farm on a large scale. The solution came in the form of partnerships they created with local large farms. Their first alliance was with Stan Pura of Mission Ranches, who was intrigued with the Goodmans' organic baby lettuce. The conventional farmer and the organic farmers struck a deal: Stan would provide additional acreage and teach the Goodmans how to farm using sophisticated farming techniques, and the Goodmans would teach Stan how to grow crops organically.[1]

Creating sales growth involves expansion. That may mean developing new products, creating new sales promotions, adding sales staff, or finding new ways to spread the word about your company and your products. One way to expand your business is by creating strategic alliances, or partnerships, with others— teaming up with other people, companies, and organizations in unique, often ingenious ways. When done well, such alliances create win-win situations for all the entities involved.

This chapter takes a look at some innovative ways that companies have partnered with others to increase their sales and promote public awareness of their businesses. Keep in mind that the alliances may have started out for one purpose and evolved in ways that offered benefits the companies weren't expecting. Some of these partnerships are grounded in socially responsible missions that weren't originally viewed as sales events or promotions but turned out to have long-term benefits for the companies.

When a business clearly makes socially responsible values part of its operations and carries that approach over into alliances it creates, increased revenue is often a result. This holistic approach builds brand loyalty and integrity, public awareness, and ultimately, profitability.

Creating alliances that help you generate revenue or put your products into effective distribution channels involves thought, action, and direction, as illustrated in this chapter's Partnership Strategies.

## PARTNERSHIP STRATEGY NUMBER ONE: Create partnerships that hold value for you as well as those with whom you are in alliance.

You may need to do some research to find alliances that are ideal for your business. The first place to look is within your community or within your supplier base. Once you have determined the type of alliance that can best serve you, find a partner that offers a natural fit. Consider what you want to achieve, what your partner wants to achieve, and how meeting these multiple goals will result in more revenue (or more beneficial distribution) for your business as it benefits your partner. Then make a list of everything you can do together.

Sometimes you will just happen upon an ideal partner. Be open to suggestions presented by someone who would like to work with you on a promotion, ad, or sales campaign. This alliance may give you a new spin on how you promote your product or allow you to present your product to a brand new customer base—customers you hadn't considered before but who might be receptive to learning more about your product.

In his book *Integrity: The Courage to Meet the Demands of Reality,* clinical psychologist Henry Cloud suggests that successful leaders possess three qualities. First, they know their field, their industry, or their discipline. Next, they are alliance builders, creating alliances that are mutually beneficial. And finally, they have the character to make these alliances work. He goes on to say that "alliances are about creating leverage to take what you do to a multiple."[2]

Taking your business to a multiple is a simple yet powerful concept. All too often small business owners feel alone in a sea of competition. If you can multiply the number of people you reach with your message about your product's benefits or the mission of your company by forming an innovative alliance, you leverage your time, your promotion dollars, and your brand awareness—all of which can increase sales or provide more effective distribution.

For many values-driven businesses, integrity is the cornerstone that helps anchor all of their socially responsible actions. And as these companies have prospered, worked through challenges, and expanded in diverse ways, collaborative relationships, in the form of partnerships, have often propelled them to greater sales and profitability.

Partnerships can also result in highly effective promotions when companies with common sales goals team up. Here is an example from Tom's of Maine that demonstrates how it has aligned its values with like-minded organizations to support projects that benefit customers and the public at large.

## *Common Good Partnerships*

Promoting its core values is internal to everything Tom's of Maine does as a company. One way it demonstrates this commitment is through common-good partnerships—alliances between a nonprofit organization, a retailer, local consumers, and Tom's of Maine. The company currently has three of these partnerships, each with its own program: Apple a Day, which promotes childhood health, specifically education about obesity; Dental Health for All, which promotes awareness, education, and action to support the forty million Americans—many of whom are children—who have no access to dental care; and River Awareness, which promotes cleaner rivers and watersheds that are the source of 50 percent of the nation's drinking water.

Tom's of Maine picks themes that are socially or environmentally consistent with the company's values and then finds partners and builds relationships. In the case of its nonprofit partners, it often pays the salaries for positions within the organization or provides up-front funding to help the organization promote its cause. In addition, Tom's of Maine always offers a way for local consumers to participate. "Most consumers aren't aware of these issues, and then, when they do become aware of them, they don't know what to do," says Tom O'Brien, chief operating officer. "A common-good partnership allows the local consumer, the community, to act on these values as well."[3]

The company brings in retailers who share its values and are concerned about the same issues. Once all the players are on board, they build a program at the retail level around a common-good event. "That's a very different way to promote your brand than just a dollar off," adds O'Brien.[4] For example, the Dental Health for All partnership involves educational events held at stores all over the country to help people learn how the health of their mouth may be linked to the health of their entire body.[5]

And do these partnerships pay off when it comes to increasing business for Tom's of Maine? According to O'Brien, the answer is a resounding yes! O'Brien says that a regular ad would generate anywhere from a 50 percent to a 100 percent increase in the company's business during the time the ad is running. "A common-good partnership, on average," he says, "will generate a 370 percent increase in our business during the time it's running—so more than a threefold increase in the bottom-line business for us." More important, O'Brien believes, is the ongoing loyalty these promotions generate. He feels partnerships like these help the company walk the talk. "Your deeds are what define you in terms of what kind of company you are. And what we've done is *every*place we spend money in the company, we've challenged ourselves to say, 'Is this dollar we spend consistent with our values?'"[6]

# PARTNERSHIP STRATEGY NUMBER TWO: Align yourself with companies that share your socially responsible goals and want to attract the same type of customer.

If you and your partner are both interested in reaching the same type of customer, you may have an opportunity to double your punch in the world of advertising and media attention. That's because you can mention each other in press releases and other publicity efforts and share advertising costs. You can also hold press events at each other's places of business or special promotions designed to attract customers to your stores. If you both attend events where you exhibit your products and do one-on-one selling, you may be able to feature your products at both your booths.

Sandra Marquardt, founder of On the Mark Public Relations in Silver Spring, Maryland, believes companies can benefit from forming a collective publicity campaign that focuses on a theme central to the business of each. This approach can be especially valuable for young companies or a burgeoning industry (e.g., organic cotton). Recently Sandra put together a campaign for twelve organic coffee importers, roasters, and retailers. "It's been interesting," she explains, "because the different companies all put in the same amount of money. Then they all get equal promotion, but they also are promoting the overall theme." This alliance enables all of the companies to pay an amount that normally wouldn't get them very far but on a collective basis creates a yearlong or a quarter-long outreach effort. The result for Sandra's clients was several large placements in major publications.[7]

In the press releases, she describes each company, what it does, and what its role is in the supply chain. Each press release has a different focus. For example, if the goal is to increase holiday sales in December, Sandra will focus on that as well as present trend information—where are sales now and what was the percent increase in sales over the last year? "Whatever kind of information I have on trends to show this is a moving train," she adds. Another critical element is providing information about where the participating companies' products can be purchased. If the release is tailored for an event, such as an industry conference, Sandra will ask the participants where their products can be found in the city where the event is held. Then when she talks to reporters, she can tell them where to find her clients' products. Sandra believes such collaborative promotions can increase sales for everyone, from importers to retailers.[8]

If you are going to team up with other companies to promote your products, it's critical that your products themselves are similar. "The focuses of the different companies cannot be too disparate," Sandra adds. "For example, it's easiest, say with organic wool, if everybody's got the same kinds of organic wool products." This factor becomes important when approaching editors so you can target one specific group (e.g., clothing versus interior design). Overall, Sandra has found this collective approach to public relations to be a valuable asset to her clients. "They get tremendous prominence in all the media materials, and then you're obviously making consumers more familiar with the good work that you're doing." And good publicity is definitely a plus when it comes to increased sales.[9]

For an example of a completely different kind of alliance, we turn to Honest Tea and a joint venture it formed with Ford Motor Company. This innovative strategy promoted both companies' brands and more socially responsible living—all over the country.

## The Great Tea Escape

In 2004, the "Great Tea Escape" promoted the Honest Tea brand and Ford's new alternative SUV, the 2005 Ford Escape Hybrid. Two of the vehicles, colorfully wrapped with Honest Tea bottle images and information about the SUV, toured the East and West Coasts to draw attention to the importance of organic foods and hybrid vehicles and their contribution to sustainability. The vehicles appeared at film festivals, concerts, Green Festivals (environmental expos), and natural food stores all over the country, and visitors were offered samples of the tea and information about the SUV. Promotions were also held with select retail partners, culminating in a sweepstakes drawing that awarded one lucky customer a Great Tea Escape vehicle.[10]

According to Seth Goldman, his company takes to heart the Chinese proverb "If we don't change the direction we are headed, we will end up where we are going." For him, partnering his relatively small company with a giant in the automotive industry gave Honest Tea a chance to travel a new path. "Both organic foods and hybrid vehicles represent a rare chance to take our society in a more sustainable direction by offering healthier choices for our customers and for the environment," he said during the promotion's launch. "Whether you're a company or a nonprofit, it is always easier to stay in the direction you are headed. It takes courage and vision to open yourself to new directions—to see things as they never were and ask, 'Why not?'"[11]

Considering the company has gone from $250,000 in sales in 1998 to a projected $14 million in 2006, it appears that Honest Tea has certainly learned how to set sail in profitable new directions.[12]

# PARTNERSHIP STRATEGY NUMBER THREE: Create partnerships with businesses or individuals that can teach you something and vice versa.

We've already demonstrated that education can be a powerful tool. If you partner with a company and show its representatives how your way of making a product or serving individuals can enhance their business, you build broader acceptance of your product, especially if it's innovative and new to the marketplace. And if your partnering organization can teach you a way to refine or improve something about your business (whether it's the manufacturing process, distribution, or a way to work with suppliers), you're the one who benefits.

Creating an alliance with a partner who may be unfamiliar with your business offers you the opportunity to educate others about your industry or mission. It's no secret that as momentum builds for an idea, more people will take interest. A trend is a good example—people catch on, like it, and accept it, and pretty soon a whole new way of doing something is created.

Our opening story highlighted Drew and Myra Goodman and how they grew their business from a 2 1/2-acre raspberry operation to a farm that now cultivates nearly 26,000 acres. This growth didn't happen overnight, and it certainly didn't happen without a great deal of education about organic farming by the Goodmans and their willingness to work cooperatively with conventional farmers in their region.

## *Creating Healthy Soil for an Entire Community*

Drew and Myra Goodman were alone in a sea of large conventional farms that had been using chemicals and toxic substances for generations. The Goodmans' determination to farm organically kept their venture growing, which created a demand for more land to farm.

After partnering with Stan Pura of Mission Ranches, the Goodmans went on to form other alliances, such as their partnership with the Tanimura and Antle farm. "What's been neat to see," says Samantha Cabaluna, senior marketing manager for Earthbound Farm, "is that even though the conventional farmers are still growing a lot of [crops] conventionally, they're growing a lot organically as well. But many of them have really learned from the organic farming side of things and have incorporated the soil management practices of organic farming into their conventional ranches."[13]

Sharing knowledge—the Goodmans' knowledge and passion for organic farming and the conventional farmers' expertise in large farming techniques—has helped propel the interest and growth in organic foods and enabled all of these farmers to reap rewards. In addition, the entire community has learned to appreciate the value of restoring the soil to organic standards (required to label food grown on the land as organic). And this may be one of the most valuable lessons in a world fraught with preservatives, toxins, and health problems linked to such chemicals.

As Samantha says of one local man who has been farming for generations. "He says, 'You think you know a lot about farming when you're this big conventional farmer, and then you start farming organically. The lands can transition, you can grow organic product after three years of transition, but the soil is just barely starting to heal itself at that point.' And he says it takes around the seven- or eight-year mark where you can really look at the soil and say, 'Now that's healthy soil.'"[14]

# PARTNERSHIP STRATEGY NUMBER FOUR: Invest in a joint venture with a technologically experienced partner.

Every business has costs. It takes money to create a product, to package it, to get it to customers, to promote it—the list could go on and on. Sometimes, investing in a new way of doing something offers real benefits if you want to differentiate your product. This may mean investing in equipment that allows you to produce more product faster or investing in higher-quality ingredients to give your end product superiority in the industry. Perhaps it's overhauling how you get your products to your customers and spending money to improve delivery times.

As you will see in our next example, it may also mean creating a new way of producing your product that better matches your socially responsible mission and at the same time gives you a higher-quality product.

# *Revamping the Process*

T.S. Designs, Inc., based in Burlington, North Carolina, was faced with a problem with respect to competing in the marketplace and fulfilling its goal of making a sustainable product that is healthy for the environment and for those who make the product. Its solution was to invest in a new technology that has completely transformed the business and how messages and illustrations are printed on T-shirts.

Founded in 1975 by Tom Sineath, T.S. Designs was built by young men with grit, energy, and determination. Tom and Eric Henry turned the textile screenprinting company into a profitable venture with 100 employees and annual revenues of close to $4 million. Their value-added proposition historically had been to produce very high-quality and innovative screenprinting services for major retail brands. They counted among their clients Nike, Polo, Reebok, and Tommy Hilfiger, and the company served as a subcontractor for major textile producers such as Vanity Fair Corporation, Sara Lee Corporation, and the William Carter Company.

In 1994, NAFTA (North American Free Trade Agreement) caused a shift in T.S. Designs' profitability when its major clients began to move apparel sourcing out of the United States to save money.[15] By 1998, the company was struggling because it was getting devastated by price. "It was either match the unbelievable cheap offshore prices or not do the business," says Eric, T.S. Designs' president. So the two entrepreneurs started to think about how they could change their business. Concerned about the environment and committed to the triple bottom line of people, planet, and profits, they came up with a way to gain a competitive edge while making a difference environmentally. Because conventional screenprinting used plastisol ink, which at that time usually contained polyvinyl chloride (PVC)—a product that can cause serious environmental and health problems because of the dioxin it generates—the partners decided to develop a technology they could control that had greater value.

Investing their own money, resources, and time, they teamed up with Burlington Chemical in North Carolina to develop and patent their Rehance technology.[16] About $250,000 later, the two companies had created a process that enabled T.S. Designs to print finished, undyed apparel product and then garment-dye it to a specified color. This process eliminates the need to invest in color inventory and allows for quick responses to unique color requests. Because the Rehance technology involves using water-based inks, garment-dyeing the finished product results in nearly zero shrinkage. Thanks to Rehance, T.S. Designs could offer a higher quality product with an improved life cycle and ecological footprint.[17]

Although the business owners had solved one part of their problem, offshore pricing was still pulling business away, and Eric and Tom had to drastically reduce the size of their operation. However, today the company is climbing toward profitability once again  by remaining true to a sustainability model. The company's T-shirts are organic cotton, and Eric is adamant about doing everything he can to put more North Carolina textile workers back to work. "Two hundred fifty thousand people just in North Carolina lost their jobs in textiles due to globalization," he points out.[18]

Today T.S. Designs creates products for companies like Clif Bar, Ben & Jerry's Ice Cream, Greenpeace, and Timberland—companies that respect T.S. Designs' commitment to sustainability and are willing to pay a higher price because of it.[19]

# PARTNERSHIP STRATEGY NUMBER FIVE: Partner with a company that has a product that can enhance your customers' lives.

Teaming up with a partner to enhance some aspect of your customers' lives while spreading the word about your business, its products, and your overall mission can result in increased sales and a larger—perhaps even new—customer base.

Consider the kinds of interests your customers may share and how you and your partner can develop a promotion that will best suit those interests. For example, if your customers are extremely interested in ways to improve the health of the environment, you will want to gear your promotion in that direction. If someone comes to you with a product that does not fit your customers' needs and interests, the promotion is likely to fail and may even create animosity toward your business.

In this next example, you'll see how two companies with similar target customers have joined forces to promote both businesses in an entertaining manner.

## Heightening the Experience

Hidden Beach Recordings and Warm Spirit have entered into a unique partnership that is enabling both companies to promote their brands to new customers. The alliance also offers Warm Spirit consultants a chance to earn extra income and special rewards and have a new tool for enhancing their business presentations.

Nadine and Hidden Beach CEO Steve McKeever met when both participated in a panel discussion in Chicago about wealth creation and the need for African Americans to work cooperatively and collaboratively together. Each was aware of the other and their companies and realized they shared the same mission: to do well by doing good. Their collaboration began simply: Hidden Beach compiled a special two-CD set of songs featuring the recording company's artists. This limited-edition CD set was made available only to Warm Spirit consultants, who could purchase it for a special price.

Plans are in the works to create other special-edition CDs that Warm Spirit consultants may use as promotional items and tie-ins to Warm Spirit product offerings. For example, a Mother's Day CD entitled *Woman First* was offered with a Warm Spirit Mother's Day product promotion Nadine created. The two CEOs have also created a CD especially designed to enhance the consultants' product and business opportunity presentations.

In addition, Nadine hopes to offer sales incentives that would give the company's consultants a chance to earn free tickets to concerts featuring Hidden Beach artists or possibly even meet the artists. The Hidden Beach-Warm Spirit partnership is designed to improve the general lifestyle of the consultants and heighten their experience as businesspeople in the Warm Spirit community. It also exposes Warm Spirit to the artists and those connected to Hidden Beach's operation. Hidden Beach, in return, gains exposure through Warm Spirit's growing consultant force.

# COLLECTIVE WISDOM

- **Make sure your values are aligned with your partner's values.** As you are developing strategic alliances with other individuals or organizations, make sure your values align so you are all working toward a common goal. Even if you want to sell more products and your partner wants to gain publicity, you should create your joint venture with the same values-driven mindset.

- **Choose alliances geared to your target market.** To make your publicity efforts effective, choose a partner that targets the same group as you do. This will save costs and avoid a shotgun approach to contacting the media.

- **Learn from others and teach others.** You can further your mission and promote your industry by collaborating with organizations that are willing to learn more about your business and willing to help you understand more about theirs.

- **Find a technologically savvy partner.** By partnering with a company that has advanced technology you can use in your business, you may find ways to create a better product or a more streamlined distribution system.

- **Enhance your customers' lives.** Find a partner who has a product that can improve your customers' lives or somehow make their lives more enjoyable. You can create goodwill and enthusiasm and use the product for special promotions.

# 7

# Celebrating achievements

## THE CREATIVE CHALLENGE: Recognizing those connected with your business so they feel good about their contributions to your organization

Sometimes it's the little things that contribute to how well your employees help your business grow. Hot Lips Pizza's David Yudkin has discovered that small perks make a big difference in creating a positive environment in his stores. Hot Lips' employees are given $30 for their birthdays, and they know their jobs will be held for them if they're employees in good standing and need to take some time off for personal reasons. Respecting other cultures is also important to David, so he's made the management systems bilingual and considers his Latino employees' interests in day-to-day operations. For example, on Cinco de Mayo, he asked his Latino employees how they would like to express their culture. The answer: a modified pizza they were proud to offer Hot Lips' customers. According to David, such employee appreciation has attracted higher-caliber "thinking people" to the business and reduces employee turnover. This means lower personnel costs and more margin for profit as Hot Lips Pizza's sales grow.[1]

In this chapter, we want to show how valuable it can be to recognize your employees (and others who may assist you) and to celebrate their accomplishments and contributions to your company's mission and growth. If you're just starting a business, such a goal may appear to be one of those "someday" objectives: *when* you have more sales coming in, *when* you're making a substantial profit and can afford really nice recognition gifts, *when* the business is more established and your staff is more experienced.

We ask you to dismiss that notion and consider making recognition and celebration a regular, robust part of your business plan from day one. Why? Because celebrating the accomplishments of those in your organization, especially those directly responsible for sales, will help build confidence, loyalty, and enthusiasm in your company. And if you're already in business, implement some changes if you have to and make recognition and celebration an integral part of your day-to-day activities. Studies indicate that companies that routinely recognize and celebrate their employees' contributions do well financially and have lower employee turnover. An added bonus is that you will create a workforce that really likes working for you. And isn't that in itself a worthy outcome?

In their book *The Invisible Employee: Realizing the Hidden Potential in Everyone,* Adrian Gostick and Chester Elton refer to a survey conducted by Sirota Consulting (cited in *Giving Employees What They Want: The Returns Are Huge,* by Louis A. Mischkind and Michael Irwin Meltzer), which reported that out of twenty-eight companies surveyed, the fourteen considered to have high morale saw their stock prices increase an average of 16 percent in 2004. The industry average for 2004 was 6 percent. And the "low morale" companies? Their stock increased an average of just 3 percent.[2]

"But my company is a small, privately held business," you say. "I'm not worried about stock value." Adrian and Chester also cite studies that reveal a direct correlation between recognition and return on equity (ROE) as well as return on assets (ROA). A survey conducted by the Jackson Group in cooperation with O.C. Tanner, an employee recognition firm based in Salt Lake City, Utah, revealed that companies committed to rewarding excellence enjoyed an ROA more than three times higher than companies that don't practice routine recognition. After all their analysis, the researchers determined that employee recognition is perhaps the one factor in regard to financial measures that most significantly impacts operating margin.[3]

To help you find recognition and celebration tech-niques that may help those connected to your business feel better about what they do, we've created some Recognition Strategies. Remember, your sales are not dependent on a simple "goods for money" transaction. Strong sales that continue to grow are built on many factors, including the loyalty and enthusiasm of those selling your products, the quality of your products, your ability to get your products to your customers in a timely fashion, and how your customers are treated by everyone in your organization. Celebrating the accomplishments of the people who are responsi-ble for these aspects of your business can make a difference in your ability to build a healthier bottom line.

# RECOGNITION STRATEGY NUMBER ONE: Use the power of the Internet and company intranet to keep in touch with your employees.

In today's high-tech age, you would be hard-pressed to find a company that doesn't use computers and the Internet to move its business forward. And while you may have created a dazzling Web site and have a sophisticated Internet system in place to handle online orders and customer inquiries, you may be overlooking the value that Internet technology can offer you internally.

As your business grows and you add more and more people to your workforce, consider developing an intranet system that will heighten communication and recognition possibilities between management and employees and also among employees themselves. An intranet provides an easy way for everyone to stay connected and gives you a method for instantly recognizing the accomplishments of your staff among their peers.

Canada's Mountain Equipment Co-op (MEC) has found a great way to give its employees a "voice," which goes a long way toward building morale, recognizing great ideas, and helping solve problems—all of which can add up to more and bigger sales.

## Talk to the Blog

Sustainability manager Denise Taschereau knows that recognition and celebration are important elements in MEC's success. And like many managers, she's always looking for novel ways to support the co-op's business efforts in these areas. "I think it's endemic that people don't celebrate enough," she says from her office in Vancouver, British Columbia. "One of the things that we've recently built is a sustainability team at MEC. We have a rep at every store that works with the team here at the head office." MEC has created its own Web-based forum, the Sustainability Center. In the form of a blog, it enables people to tell others within the company about events they've held and to do a little bragging. As Denise explains, "It's been a really nice way for people in a really short, quick forum, to say, 'We did this. It worked!'"[4]

Once items are posted on the blog, Denise can easily search the site and forward information to the senior vice presidents so they know what's happening in the co-op. In addition to posting "successes," the Sustainability team can seek solutions to problems or ask questions that may pop up. A case in point is excess packaging from the boats the co-op sells. Someone asked for suggestions for what to do with all the plastic wrapping used to protect the boats when they're shipped, and the answers were quick to come in. One person at an MEC store gives the packaging to an eBay seller who reuses it when shipping items. Another cuts the plastic into sections  and gives it away to customers to use as ground sheets for tents. The Sustainability Center site also  allows staff members to vent if faced with a challenging issue. Denise believes this communication forum is a valuable asset to the company, whether it's to celebrate, to recognize, or just simply to communicate.[5]

As this example demonstrates, allowing your employees to share successes and seek solutions to problems via your intranet is a great way for everyone involved in your day-to-day operation to connect. And being connected helps build teamwork, which can be critical when trying to come up with new ideas for increasing your sales or solving distribution issues.

## RECOGNITION STRATEGY NUMBER TWO: Find innovative ways to recognize and reward your employees by tapping into their personal interests.

Every person in the universe has a talent or interest that is unique. Sometimes it takes just a little effort to find out what that interest is and then to recognize it to make your employees feel special. And what does making your staff feel special have to do with sales and distribution? The answer is simple: making people feel good about themselves creates a positive atmosphere. And a positive atmosphere can generate more energy and cooperation in the workplace, which can translate into more productivity and sales.

In *The Invisible Employee,* Gostick and Elton point out that sometimes the most important time to celebrate is when it appears nothing is worthy of celebration.[6] When you're experiencing a slump in sales or challenges getting products to customers in a timely  fashion, could be the time you need real ingenuity and a chance to celebrate suggested solutions.

Tapping into your employees' interests and recognizing them for their talents can be a wonderful way to get their creative juices flowing and get them feeling more relaxed about offering valuable input into ways to improve your operation. If you're willing to listen and have a sincere desire to help your employees live a better life through your actions as an employer, you may discover a host of new ideas that put sales on a profitable track or save money in getting products to customers. And as Albert Einstein said, "Logic will get you from A to B. Imagination will take you every-where."[7]

You don't have to spend a lot, in either time or money, to give your employees a boost in how they feel about themselves and how they feel about working for you. In the following example, we show you how MEC combines supporting its mission as a company with supporting its employees' personal interests.

# The Value of Rewards

MEC rewards its employees through programs that benefit them on a personal level in a way that matches the co-op's mission. The co-op recently launched a boat/bike loan program that enables full- or part-time employees who have been with MEC for over a year to take out an interest-free loan up to Can$3,000. Employees may buy a canoe, kayak, mountain bike, road bike—whatever they want—and the interest-free payments are deducted from their paychecks over a two-year period. This program helps employees enjoy some of the recreational activities MEC supports as a business, and it encourages interest in such hobbies, which can make MEC employees more knowledgeable and more enthusiastic about helping customers interested in the same activities.

The organization does a lot of in-the-field staff training, which Denise says not only provides valuable instruction but also is enjoyable for employees. "A group of staff can sign up to go to an Avalanche Awareness course for two or three days and be [trained] in the mountains," she explains. Such trainings help build expertise on the floor when employees are dealing with MEC members, plus they're fun and give staff members a break from the usual routine in the store. In addition to these methods of helping employees become more familiar with and passionate about outdoor recreation, by 2007

MEC hopes to launch a program in which employees may volunteer to work for an organization of their choice on company time. This is another example of how the business enhances its mission through supporting its employees.[8]

One other way the co-op recognizes its employees is through its order line on-hold music. We've all been put on hold and often hear music while we wait for someone to help us. What is unique about MEC's on-hold music is its source—the music is composed and performed by an MEC staff member. How do you know that? Because a woman announces this fact. When Angela called MEC's 800 number and heard this, her immediate reaction was "How cool!" And then she thought, How easy to do! Why aren't more companies doing this?

According to Harry Henderson, MEC service center manager, this unique foray into employee recognition came about because the co-op wasn't happy with the corporate music and messaging service it was purchasing. Customers and staff members complained that the music just didn't fit the MEC culture. And when someone on staff said employee musicians could do a better job, the company agreed. Besides the employee musicians, the woman who does the announcing (in both English and French) is also an MEC employee.[9]

If you examine the employee rolls of most companies, especially large ones like MEC, you will no doubt discover a number of artists, writers, and musicians who spend much of their free time nurturing an artistic passion. And any talent agent can tell you how tough it is for an artist, writer, or musician to get his or her work before the public, whether it's a gallery showing of artwork, a book published, or a music CD produced.

Why not allow talented employees to showcase their talent where they work and brighten your environment at the same time? For example, in addition to musicians supplying your on-hold music, artists could submit works of art for lobbies or other areas in your building where people gather or pass by regularly.

Your first step in creating such programs may be to find out what your employees are interested in and how their interests could be showcased. It all comes back to appreciating people and making them feel good about their job and working for the benefit of your company. If your employees enjoy being part of your company, chances are that enthusiasm will reveal itself when they encounter customers or others who play a role in your success, including suppliers, distributors, the media, and potential investors. Selling your merchandise often begins with selling the spirit of your values and company mission to those who are on your front line—i.e., your employees.

# RECOGNITION STRATEGY NUMBER THREE: Find small ways to reward your employees.

If you think it's strictly the paycheck that keeps your employees showing up for work every day, think again. Your ability to lead plays a significant role. It's no secret that good leaders can guide their teams to amazing heights of success. Part of being a good leader is understanding the challenges your employees may face in their personal lives and finding ways to work with them to help improve their quality of life and, thus, their ability to do their jobs. It really boils down to making it easy for your employees to like working for you. And consideration for your employees today can mean payoffs tomorrow when you have a business crisis (e.g., you have pallets of products that have to be unloaded in a hurry, and you need employees to stay late).

In our opening example, we highlighted a few ways that Hot Lips Pizza does little things to help its employees enjoy their work and feel appreciated for their efforts. Here are some other actions David Yudkin takes to give his business a strong sense of community (integral to his mission) as he builds respectful relationships with those connected to his business.

# *As Much Pizza as They Can Stand*

One way you can see how Hot Lips recognizes people is by going to its Web site. There you'll see a photo of the local farmers who supply Hot Lips with the ingredients for its pizzas and homemade soda. It's a nice way to recognize these members of David's community who help him make quality pizza and original soda. And in the case of the soda, David also uses the name of the farm on the soda labels if all the fruit comes from that one particular farm.

Does it cost David anything extra to feature the farmers on his Web site or use their names on a soda label? No. Does it mean something? You bet. According to David, the farmers love it. And will this appreciation for their contributions to Hot Lips Pizza show itself when a problem erupts and a supplier has to go that extra mile to get David the produce or flour he needs? Very likely. And as any business owner will tell you, having the ingredients or parts you need *when* you need them is essential to fostering healthy sales. It all goes back to creating a quality product and giving customers what they want when they want it.

In addition to celebrating employees' birthdays and appreciating their cultures, David makes an effort to train his employees so they will understand the nature of his business. Because Hot Lips uses fresh, locally grown (and often organic) produce—which of course is seasonal—it's critical that his employees know why some ingredients may not be available for a customer's pizza and can therefore relate that information confidently to customers. They also learn the meaning of "organic" and "sustainability" and the various ways Hot Lips Pizza works to lower its impact on the environment. "When an employee is supporting their job in that kind of way, they are happier! And it lowers turnover," adds David.[10]

Another way David tries to keep his employees happy is by offering flexible work schedules and vacation pay no matter what level job they have. David is also working on a volunteer program so employees can volunteer up to three hours a month, for which they will receive one hour of pay. And he adds, "They can eat as much pizza as they can stand."[11]

Gift certificates are a staple at Hot Lips—for going beyond the call of duty or just for brightening up a bad day. David even let a music-loving employee negotiate a deal with a local record store so he can select the music to play in the stores. Another employee loves hot sauce, so he helped the company create a hot sauce to market. All of these perks are small compared to the huge bonuses some companies pay, but for a small operation they can be monumental when it comes to creating and nurturing a satisfied workforce.

David has found that these actions attract employees who want to have an impact in the community or on the world and are concerned about environmental issues. In short, he feels they come to work because they feel like they can play a role in changing the world.[12]

All of this gives David the "thinking people" we mentioned earlier. And when the people working for you embrace your values, their enthusiasm radiates to those they encounter as they do their jobs. If those people are customers, you have a much better chance to sell your product the first time around and resell it over and over again. Your employees' enthusiasm will also radiate to people they meet away from the job, which can add up to new customers and more sales.

# RECOGNITION STRATEGY NUMBER FOUR: If your company's revenue depends on a large sales force, create a rewarding recognition program.

Your company may depend on a sales force to sell your products. If so, it's important to create a recognition program that offers your salespeople incentives that they appreciate and that motivate them. Two direct-selling companies that depend on a large core of salespeople to tell their story and sell products are Warm Spirit and Nu Skin Enterprises. Both organizations have created recognition programs that play a critical role in improving sales and spreading the word about their companies. These programs highlight the individuals' success among their peers and the public at large, which in turn helps motivate the award recipients to meet new goals. Simply put, it's the old concept of rewarding behaviors you want repeated.

However, for both Warm Spirit and Nu Skin Enterprises, recognition is far more complex and sophisticated than merely handing out a gift when a distributor or consultant reaches a new level of achievement. And even though you may have a small company that is not dependent on high sales volumes generated by thousands of individuals, the techniques these companies use may give you ideas for improving your own sales efforts.

First, here's a little primer on the direct-selling model. Although compensation plans and requirements to qualify for advancement differ among companies, the basic direct-selling model (often called network marketing) involves selling products and the business opportunity to other individuals. Distributors (Warm Spirit calls them consultants) may elect to just sell products at a suggested retail price (and earn income on the markup) or to create an organization of their own by signing up other individuals who will both sell products and recruit new individuals into the business. As individuals recruit more and more people into the business, they earn commissions as well as bonuses, depending on the size of their organization and the total sales volume generated by everyone in their group. For successful distributors who work hard and recruit many active distributors into their organization, incomes can be huge. And of course, since individual incomes are based on sales, those earning regular, large commissions are generating significant income for the company.

Nu Skin Enterprises, based in Provo, Utah, was founded in 1984 as a personal care company. Today it operates three divisions and spans the globe, with approximately 800,000 distributors in over forty markets.[13] In this next example, you'll see how the company grew by consistently celebrating the efforts of its sales force—often in small but creative ways.

## *Rolling Out the Red Carpet*

From the beginning, Nu Skin put an emphasis on recognizing its leaders. They're highlighted in company publications, featured on the lobby walls in the corporate office as well as in their individual market offices, and feted at regional conferences as well as the corporation's large international convention held every two years in the United States, and they earn exclusive trips and gifts as they reach new levels within the company. Although Nu Skin rewards its top leaders handsomely, the "little things" often seem to carry significant weight. This is a valuable lesson for any business, no matter how small.

"It's interesting to see what recognition really does—what motivates people," says Nu Skin Enterprises' director of global recognition, Darin Ashby. "We've had people who were more concerned about their title and didn't really care what the check was." Further evidence that the little things support big results can be found in the pillow gifts Darin and his team leave for their top leaders, called Team Elite members, on their annual trips. These are small gifts such as towels, shirts, jackets, umbrellas, water bottles, or even a kite. One year, due to a lack of storage space, the recognition team did not give the leaders pillow gifts on their Alaskan cruise. And did they ever hear about it! "Those things cost as little as ten dollars apiece," says Darin. "Several of these people are millionaires—a good share of them. They could buy the company that makes those trinkets, you know? But they've got to have that little gift ... Just taking extra care with every aspect of these trips, it's really motivating to them. It blows them away. They haven't had service or recognition like that—ever."[14]

Nu Skin also recognizes its sales leaders through another very simple, low-cost activity. As individuals reach certain milestones within the company, they are brought to corporate headquarters to meet with company executives and are taken on fun outings. On their first morning in Provo, they are bussed as a group from the hotel to the company's downtown high-rise, and there they are routinely astounded by what awaits them: a red carpet, celebratory music, and hundreds of corporate employees who applaud their entrance into the building. "A lot of them say it's the highlight of their trip," says Darin, "feeling like royalty."[15]

For Nu Skin Enterprises, which has helped over 350 people earn over $1 million during the lifetime of their distributorship and 20 to earn over $20 million, recognition has been a very significant part of how the company does business and keeps sales moving upward. As Darin says, "Recognition is the name of the game in direct sales."[16]

## Shining Stars

Nadine also knows that direct selling is a business based on recognition, and she has instituted several programs that not only recognize her consultants but help them do their jobs better at the same time. Every month the company recognizes the top nine people, who are its Shining Stars. These consultants receive a nice gift or gift certificate, are highlighted in the company's monthly newsletter and in an e-mail sent to all consultants, and are noted on the public Internet site as well as the company intranet site. They also receive mention in a press release sent to their local media by a public relations firm that specializes in publicizing the accomplishments of direct-selling representatives. This press release serves two purposes: it provides local recognition of consultants' efforts and helps consultants publicize their businesses in their communities to aid them in making more product sales and attracting new recruits.

The final piece of the recognition program for Warm Spirit's top earners is the three hours of coaching they receive the month following their Shining Star status. These consultants receive an hour each of life coaching, self-care and wellness coaching, and leadership training. The thinking behind this program is to let the consultants know that the company appreciates their leadership efforts and is willing to invest three hours of coaching time in them to help take them and their business to the next level.

$$***$$

In all of these examples, we've demonstrated how recognizing a person's contribution to your company—whether through his or her ideas, work performance, or commitment to your goals as a business—can help you realize a more profitable bottom line. In addition, we've shown you how recognizing people's talents, interests, or simple needs in managing an often-hectic life can help them feel better about who they are and therefore probably do a better job as an employee.

It all boils down to one simple idea: if people are happy and feel appreciated, they're going to feel good about coming to work, pitching in during tough times, and offering new ideas when you want to inject some energy into your sales. They'll sell with more fervor and with a genuine passion for what they're selling, and they'll be more effective ambassadors when talking about their jobs and your company to friends or strangers they may meet when they're not at work. By celebrating the contributions of those connected to your business, you create a more positive atmosphere that can definitely add up to bigger profits.

---

## COLLECTIVE WISDOM

• **Create a forum for employee communication.** Use the power of technology to create a quick and easy way for your employees to highlight their accomplishments, ask questions, and offer solutions to one another when problems arise. This will make them feel connected and important to your operation.

• **Highlight your employees' personal interests.** Find ways to showcase your employees' talents and interests. This will help make them feel appreciated as individuals and create a more enjoyable environment for them and possibly for everyone connected to your business.

• **Show appreciation in small ways.** When it comes to employee retention and dedication, the little things can add up. You may want to start by asking your employees what kinds of policies would be most beneficial to them—e.g., flextime schedules, paid volunteer hours, incentives for meeting work-related goals.

• **Celebrate sales goals.** In addition to bonuses and other sales rewards, consider ways you can train your sales force as you recognize them. And remember that even small gestures of appreciation can be motivating to those who are responsible for making big sales.

# 8

# Do values really sell?

Throughout this book we have cited companies and individuals that have found ways to build sales or create effective distribution strategies while maintaining their core values and socially responsible missions. Some of these companies have proven financial track records and years of experience or have sold for many millions of dollars. Others are newer to the world of business and are striving each year to reach their financial goals.

We believe that creating a business built on a foundation of values can not only increase sales in the short term but also build long-term benefits. This is a premise that many people, especially those reading a book like this, would heartily embrace. However, certainly some in the business world might argue that such an idea is purely idealistic.

As we started working on this book, Angela discussed the subject of social responsibility (and what was involved in creating the contents for this project) with her twenty-three-year-old son, Ryan. Savvy and a true philosopher at heart, he asked her a simple question: Why should a business be socially responsible? Good question, she reasoned, especially since socially responsible actions can include developing a more expensive product, limiting your distribution channel, paying higher salaries or commissions, and donating a portion of your profits to a worthwhile cause—actions that could bite into your bottom line from a purely revenue point of view. Some people might contend that it makes more sense to be as profitable as possible as quickly as possible and then do good for society with the money you've earned. Many companies have done that over the years, much to society's benefit.

To help us answer the question and pinpoint why it does make good revenue-building sense to be socially responsible, Nadine spoke with Derek Taylor, CEO of Global Solutions Group USA. Derek is well versed in financial management, Securities and Exchange Commission reporting, and Sarbanes-Oxley compliance and risk management. He is also the designer of "Budget Management Training for Non Profit Managers," a program that guides participants in developing world-class solutions to real-world problems.[1]

Derek believes that if companies abandon socially responsible ideals and do whatever it takes to keep profits high, their actions will eventually hit their bottom line in a negative way. He cites the recent spate of scandals that have toppled huge corporations and hurt the standing of companies that are still in business but are now trying to correct their actions—sometimes at great expense.

To create sustainable relationships, a business must do well by doing good because customers choose where they want to spend their dollars. And a strong relationship with your community is one of the best relationships a business can forge, Derek believes.[2] That's because your community can support you when times are tough—a fact David Yudkin of Hot Lips Pizza discovered when he and his wife were restructuring the business and struggling to pay off the previous owners' sizable debt. Throughout this difficult period people within the community continued to give Hop Lips their business. By becoming a good corporate citizen in your community first, you recycle money back into your community. This fosters loyalty to your business among local citizens—customers who can support you in the long run. And you can expand this "doing well by doing good" philosophy beyond your community as your business grows.

Warm Spirit has experienced this expansion of social responsibility as more and more consultants joined the business and created their own communities throughout the United States. In addition, Nadine has contracted with minority- and women-owned vendors to supply the company with many of its products, thereby helping these small businesses grow and become more successful. And now she is reaching out to other parts of the world by using the company's mission of empowerment to support women in Northern Ghana. Nadine recently began purchasing shea butter, used in many Warm Spirit products, from a women's cooperative in the region. Profits earned by these women are then used to support education and health initiatives in their communities.

The real crux of the issue may be a simple matter of building long-term integrity—coupled with financial stability—versus seeking short-term financial gains. You've learned from businesses like Tweezerman, Tom's of Maine, Imagine Foods, French Meadow Bakery, and Birkenstock USA that operating a business in a socially responsible manner can lead to increased sales, strong and effective alliances, and even lucrative company buyouts. And no one is espousing doing poorly financially just so you can be a good corporate citizen. What the companies featured in this work and many other companies throughout the world demonstrate is that you can create a business with strong core values that support social responsibility, be innovative in your strategies to build sales and form powerful distribution channels, and come out a winner on many levels: by succeeding financially, by furthering your mission within your industry, and by improving society as a whole.

None of us can change the world single-handedly in one fell swoop. However, each of us can contribute to making the world a better place. That's what these companies are demonstrating time and time again, often with creative sales campaigns or innovative alliances—even basic day-to-day operating policies—that contribute to how well they sell their products or get them to their customers. And each time they experience revenue growth and expand into a new market, they are telling the world that values can make a difference.

Paulette Cole, CEO and creative director of ABC Home Furnishings (part of ABC Carpet & Home), is a businesswoman who understands and embraces this philosophy, even after many years of success without practicing sustainability and promoting conscious consumerism. She realizes it will take effort to transform ABC Home Furnishings into a socially responsible business. As she points out, when you're starting a business, you can build it from the ground  up and make certain choices about how you want to operate that business—how you want to define your story. For an established store like ABC Home Furnishings, it's all about transitioning and finding  products to match the store's high expectations of beauty while retaining as much as possible of the indigenous "DNA" of the products' design and practicing sustainability. But Paulette is confident that social responsibility's time has come. "From my point of view, investing in social responsibility and opening businesses that are socially responsible will be a lucrative direction for many businesses—all businesses I should think. It's the way of the future. I think that all the designers will be encouraged to design product that is not only great product but that is in service to the earth. Because we can't be antithetically opposed anymore. It just doesn't make sense, you know?"[3]

To answer Ryan's question, we believe that operating a business with a socially responsible mission is good business. It fosters awareness of issues affecting communities and the world as a whole, which ultimately can help businesses to be valuable contributors toward making the world a better place. And as these businesses help improve society, they become more successful in the marketplace because customers—the people buying their products—respect what they're doing.

We're betting that more and more businesses—new and established alike—will indeed see the wisdom in using their values as their guide to increased sales and profits, that they will recognize the benefits of supporting their communities, empowering and recognizing their employees, developing strategic alliances with like-minded individuals and organizations, educating others about their product and mission, and continuing to find new customers by keeping their visions firmly in sight. And most of all, we believe they will understand that not only do values matter when it comes to building a business, values *sell.*

# Notes

## Chapter 1

[1]   Danny Quintana, interview by author, Salt Lake City, UT, May 10, 2006.

[2]   Jeff Mendelsohn, phone interview by author, February 16, 2006.

[3]   Ibid.

[4]   Ibid.

[5]   New Leaf Paper, "Welcome to NewLeafPaper.com," http://www.newleafpaper.com/index.html (accessed February 13, 2006).

[6]   David Yudkin, phone interview by author, May 10, 2006; and Businesses for an Environmentally Sustainable Tomorrow, "Hot Lips Awarded for Energy Efficiency," http://www.sustainableportland.org/stp_BEST.html (accessed May 9, 2006).

[7]   David Yudkin, phone interview by author, May 10, 2006.

[8]   Ibid.

[9]   Jeffrey Hollender, phone interview by author, February 14, 2006.

[10]  Jeffrey Hollender and Stephen Fenichell, *What Matters Most: How a Small Group of Pioneers Is Teaching Social Responsibility to Big Business, and Why Big Business Is Listening* (New York: Basic Books, 2004), x.

[11]  Jeffrey Hollender, phone interview by author, February 14, 2006.

[12]  Ibid.

[13]    Ibid.

[14]    Tom's of Maine, "What Is Natural Care?" http://www.tomsofmaine.com/about/natural_care.asp (accessed April 17, 2006).

[15]    Tom's of Maine, "Tom and Kate Chappell Announce Partnership with Colgate," http://tomsofmaine.com/about/Colgate.asp (accessed July 25, 2006).

[16]    Tom O'Brien, phone interview by author, April 24, 2006.

[17]    Ibid.

## Chapter 2

[1]    Honest Tea, "Our Story: We Were Thirsty," http://www.honesttea.com/our_story/content.html (accessed April 4, 2006).

[2]    Samuel Fromatz, "Greener Tea," *Forbes Small Business,* April 2005, 86, 88.

[3]    Honest Tea, "Honest Tea Launches the First Unsweetened Organic Ready-to-Drink Tea," http://honesttea.com/news/pressrelease36.html (accessed April 25, 2006).

[4]    Ibid.

[5]    Ibid.

[6]    Seth Goldman, phone interview by author, April 25, 2006.

[7]    Birkenstock, "History," http://www.birkenstockusa.com/our_company/history/ (accessed April 4, 2006).

[8]    Margot Fraser, phone interview by author, April 4, 2006.

[9]    Ibid.

[10]    Ibid.

[11]    Ibid.

[12]    Ibid.

[13]    Link TV, "Background," http://www.linktv.org/about/background.php3 (accessed April 9, 2006).

[14]    Ray Richmond, "Link TV Finding Audience with 'Mosaic,'" *Hollywood Reporter,* April 21, 2005, http://linktv.org/press/pdf/Hlywd_Rptr4_21_05.pdf (accessed April 9, 2006).

[15]    Ibid.

[16]    Link TV, "Mission," http://worldlinktv.com/about/mission.php3 (accessed April 9, 2006).

[17]    Ray Richmond, "Link TV Finding Audience with 'Mosaic,'" *Hollywood Reporter,* April 21, 2005, http://linktv.org/press/pdf/Hlywd_Rptr4_21_05.pdf (accessed April 9, 2006).

[18]    Ibid.

[19]    Kim Spencer, phone interview by author, March 9, 2006.

[20]    Ibid; and Michael B. Soper, TeamSoper.Com, obtained from Target Analysis Inc., National donor Centrics Report, 2004, e-mail message to author, April 9, 2006.

[21]    Kim Spencer, e-mail message to author, May 1, 2006.

[22]    Kim Spencer, phone interview by author, March 9, 2006.

[23]   Dan Storper, phone interview by author, March 23, 2006.

[24]   Ibid.

[25]   Ibid.

# Chapter 3

[1]   Lynn Gordon, phone interview by author, August 25, 2006.

[2]   Kunmi Oluleye, phone interview by author, September 4, 2006.

[3]   Ibid.

[4]   Ibid.

[5]   Kellie McElhaney, phone interview by author, August 28, 2006.

[6]   Ibid.

[7]   Kopali Organics, "Our Human Mission," http://kopaliorganics.com/node/68 (accessed August 31, 2006).

[8]   Kopali Organics, "Our History," http://kopaliorganics.com/node/64 (accessed August 31, 2006).

[9]   Zak Zaidman, phone interview by author, August 23, 2006.

[10]   Kellie McElhaney, phone interview by author, August 28, 2006.

[11]   Ibid.

[12]   Lynn Gordon, phone interview by author, August 25, 2006.

[13]   Ibid.

[14]   Ibid.

[15]   Ibid.

[16]    Robert Nissenbaum, phone interview by author, August 25, 2006.
[17]    Ibid.
[18]    David Van Seters, phone interview by author, September 1, 2006.
[19]    Ibid.
[20]    Ibid.
[21]    Samantha Cabaluna, phone interview by author, April 21, 2006.
[22]    Ibid.
[23]    Myra Goodman, e-mail message to author from Samantha Cabaluna, September 8, 2006.
[24]    Samantha Cabaluna, phone interview by author, April 21, 2006.
[25]    Dancing Deer Baking Company, "How We Think," http://dancingdeer.com/howwethink2. html (accessed July 24, 2006).

## Chapter 4

[1]    Dal LaMagna, phone interview by author, March 1, 2006.
[2]    Indigenous Designs, "History," http://www.indi genousdesigns.com/history.html (accessed April 10, 2006).
[3]    Indigenous Designs, "Investors Page," http://w ww.indigenousdesigns.com/learn_more2.html (accessed April 10, 2006).
[4]    Scott Leonard, phone interview by author, April 12, 2006.
[5]    Ibid.

[6] Indigenous Designs, "Investors Page," http://www.indigenousdesigns.com/learn_more3.html (accessed April 10, 2006).

[7] Daniel Grossman, phone interview by author, April 4, 2006.

[8] Ibid.

[9] Wild Planet Toys, "Kid Inventor Challenge," http://www.kidinventorchallenge.com/ (accessed April 12, 2006).

[10] Wild Planet Toys, "About Us," http://www.wildplanet.com/aboutus/top_info.php (accessed April 12, 2006).

[11] Daniel Grossman, phone interview by author, April 4, 2006.

[12] Steve McKeever, biography, e-mailed to author by Denise McIver, April 13, 2006.

[13] Steve McKeever, phone interview by author, April 13, 2006.

[14] Ibid.

[15] Ibid.

[16] Dal LaMagna, phone interview by author, March 1, 2006.

[17] Ibid.

[18] Ibid.

[19] Ibid.

[20] Ibid.

[21] Ibid.

[22] Ibid.

[23] Ibid.

[24] Ibid.

[25]    Ibid.

# Chapter 5

[1]    Joy Maples, phone interview by author, April 26, 2006.

[2]    Mountain Equipment Co-op, "About Mountain Equipment Co-op," http://www.mec.ca/Main/content_text.jsp?FOLDER%3C%Efolder_id=1408474396038657&FOLDER%3C% (accessed May 3, 2006).

[3]    Peter ter Weeme, phone interview by author, April 24, 2006. Subsequent to this interview, Peter ter Weeme left MEC and returned to the values-based service company that he cofounded more than ten years ago.

[4]    Ibid.

[5]    Ibid.

[6]    Ibid.

[7]    Scott Mayhew, phone interview by author, April 25, 2006.

[8]    Dal LaMagna, phone interview by author, March 1, 2006.

[9]    Ibid.

[10]    Ibid.

[11]    Dave Knutson, phone interview by author, April 21, 2006.

[12]    Ibid.

[13]    Ibid.

[14]    Ibid.

[15]    Joy Maples, phone interview by author, April 26, 2006.

# Chapter 6

[1]   Samantha Cabaluna, phone interview by author, April 21, 2006.

[2]   Henry Cloud, *Integrity: The Courage to Meet the Demands of Reality* (New York: Harper Collins, 2006), 4-6.

[3]   Tom O'Brien, phone interview by author, April 24, 2006.

[4]   Ibid.

[5]   Tom's of Maine, "Tom's of Maine Events," http://www.tomsofmaine.com/about/events.asp (accessed April 24, 2006).

[6]   Tom O'Brien, phone interview by author, April 24, 2006.

[7]   Sandra Marquardt, phone interview by author, April 24, 2006.

[8]   Ibid.

[9]   Ibid.

[10]   Honest Tea, "Ford Escape Hybrid and Honest Tea Join Forces for 'The Great Tea Escape' This Summer," http://www.honesttea.com/news/pressrelease26.html (accessed April 25, 2006).

[11]   Seth Goldman, speech given at the launch of the Great Tea Escape, provided to author by e-mail, April 25, 2006.

[12]   Seth Goldman, phone interview by author, April 25, 2006.

[13]   Samantha Cabaluna, phone interview by author, April 21, 2006.

[14]   Ibid.

[15]     Eric Henry, "Manufacturing and Selling a $4.00 T-shirt in a $1.00 World," http://www.tsdesig ns.com/pdf/Manufactoring%20and%20Selling %20a%20four%20dollar%20t-shirt%20GOI% 2003.pdf (accessed April 20, 2006).

[16]     Eric Henry, phone interview by author, April 20, 2006.

[17]     Eric Henry, "Manufacturing and Selling a $4.00 T-shirt in a $1.00 World," http://www.tsdesig ns.com/pdf/Manufactoring%20and%20Selling %20a%20four%20dollar%20t-shirt%20GOI% 2003.pdf (accessed April 20, 2006).

[18]     Eric Henry, phone interview by author, April 20, 2006.

[19]     Eric Henry, "Manufacturing and Selling a $4.00 T-shirt in a $1.00 World," http://www.tsdesig ns.com/pdf/Manufactoring%20and%20Selling %20a%20four%20dollar%20t-shirt%20GOI% 2003.pdf (accessed April 20, 2006).

# Chapter 7

[1]     David Yudkin, phone interview by author, May 10, 2006.

[2]     Adrian Gostick and Chester Elton, *The Invisible Employee: Realizing the Hidden Potential in Everyone* (Hoboken, NJ: John Wiley & Sons, 2006), 118.

[3]     Ibid. 118-120.

[4]     Denise Taschereau, phone interview by author, May 8, 2006.

[5]     Ibid.

[6]     Adrian Gostick and Chester Elton, *The Invisible Employee: Realizing the Hidden Potential in Everyone* (Hoboken, NJ: John Wiley & Sons, 2006), 135.

[7]     Thinkexist.com, http://en.thinkexist.com/quotes/Albert_Einstein/ (accessed May 15, 2006).

[8]     Denise Taschereau, phone interview by author, May 8, 2006.

[9]     Harry Henderson, phone interview by author, May 16, 2006.

[10]    David Yudkin, phone interview by author, May 10, 2006.

[11]    Ibid.

[12]    Ibid.

[13]    Nu Skin Enterprises, http://www.nuskinenterprises.com/corp/index.shtml.

[14]    Darin Ashby, phone interview by author, May 23, 2006.

[15]    Ibid.

[16]    Ibid.

# Chapter 8

[1]     Alliance Training and Consulting, Inc., "Derek Taylor," http://www.alliancetac.com/index.html?PAGE_ID=278 (accessed September 4, 2006).

[2]     Derek Taylor, phone interview by author, August 28, 2006.

[3]     Paulette Cole, phone interview by author, May 4, 2006.

# Resources

Following is a list of Web sites you can visit to learn more about the socially responsible businesses and organizations featured in this book. By becoming familiar with their operations, you may come up with some new ideas of your own for using creativity to build strong sales and more beneficial distribution channels.

ABC Carpet & Home
(http://www.abchome.com)

Alliance Training and Consulting, Inc.
(www.alliancetac.com)

Birkenstock USA
(http://www.birkenstockusa.com)

Chaco, Inc.
(http://www.chacousa.com)

Corsair Studio
(http://www.corsairstudio.com)

Dancing Deer Baking Company
(http://www.dancingdeer.com)

Earthbound Farm
(http://www.ebfarm.com)

Earth Creations
(http://www.earthcreations.net)

French Meadow Bakery & Cafe
(http://www.frenchmeadow.com)

Haas School of Business at UC Berkeley
(http://www.haas.berkeley.edu)

Hidden Beach Recordings
(http://www.hiddenbeach.com)

Honest Tea
(http://www.honesttea.com)

Hot Lips Pizza
(http://www.hotlipspizza.com)

Imagine Foods
(http://www.imaginefoods.com)

Indigenous Designs Corporation
(http://www.indigenousdesigns.com)

Kopali Organics
(http://www.kopaliorganics.com)

Link TV
(http://www.linktv.org)

Mountain Equipment Co-op
(http://www.mec.ca)

New Leaf Paper
(http://www.newleafpaper.com)

Nu Skin Enterprises
(http://www.nuskinenterprises.com)

On the Mark Public Relations
(http://www.onthemarkpr.com)

Putumayo World Music
(http://www.putumayo.com)

Seventh Generation
(http://www.seventhgeneration.com)

Sheba Foods
(http://www.shebafoods.com)

Small Potatoes Urban Delivery
(http://www.spud.ca)

Tom's of Maine
(http://www.tomsofmaine.com)

T.S. Designs
(http://www.tsdesigns.com)

Tweezerman
(http://www.tweezerman.com)

Warm Spirit
(http://www.warmspirit.com)

Wild Planet
(http://www.wildplanet.com)

# Suggested Reading

Anderson, Ray C. *Mid-Course Correction: Toward a Sustainable Enterprise—The Interface Model.* White River Junction, VT: Chelsea Green, 1998.

Arena, Christine. *Cause for Success: 10 Companies That Put Profits Second and Came in First.* Novato, CA: New World Library, 2004.

Castle, Victoria. *The Trance of Scarcity: Stop Holding Your Breath and Start Living Your Life.* San Francisco: Berrett Koehler, 2007.

Cloud, Henry. *Integrity: The Courage to Meet the Demands of Reality.* New York: Harper Collins Publishers, 2006.

Gostick, Adrian, and Chester Elton. *The Invisible Employee: Realizing the Hidden Potential in Everyone.* Hoboken, NJ: John Wiley & Sons, 2006.

Hollender, Jeffrey, and Stephen Fenichell. *What Matters Most: How a Small Group of Pioneers Is Teaching Social Responsibility to Big Business, and Why Big Business Is Listening.* New York: Basic Books, 2004.

# About Social Venture Network

SVN transforms the way the world does business by connecting, leveraging, and promoting a global community of leaders for a more just and sustainable economy.

Since its founding in 1987, SVN has grown from a handful of visionary individuals into a vibrant community of more than 400 business owners, investors, and nonprofit leaders who are advancing the movement for social responsibility in business. SVN members believe in a new bottom line for business, one that values healthy communities and the human spirit as well as high returns.

As a network, SVN facilitates partnerships, strategic alliances, and other ventures that promote social and economic justice. SVN compiles and promotes best practices for socially responsible enterprises and produces unique conferences that support the professional and personal development of business leaders and social entrepreneurs.

Please visit http://www.svn.org for more information on SVN membership, initiatives, and events.

# About the Authors

**Nadine A. Thompson** is not only the president, CEO, and cofounder of Warm Spirit, she is the visionary and leader of a community of over 20,000 women and men who are empowered entrepreneurs and change agents. In 1997, Nadine founded Warm Spirit with friend and entrepreneur Daniel Wolf. She was excited about the possibilities of creating a business venture that would enlighten and empower women. Warm Spirit provides access to entrepreneurial opportunities and high-quality natural products and creates wealth for the consultants and their communities. Its unique marketing plan returns approximately fifty cents from each dollar in sales back into the pockets of the consultants and therefore recycles wealth and profits directly back into these communities. In 2006, the company was named the Emerging Company of the Year by *Black Enterprise* magazine.

Born in Trinidad and raised in Toronto, Canada, Nadine received her masters in social work from Smith College. She went on to become dean of multicultural affairs at Phillips Exeter Academy in New Hampshire, where her rare combination of insight, cosmopolitan warmth, and a gift for bringing people together helped meld the prep school's long tradition of education with a racially diverse and representative student body and faculty. Nadine has published essays on diversity and personality and received the Onyx Woman Economic

Empowerment Award for her commitment to advancing women in the areas of entrepreneurship and personal financial growth. She is also the beauty anchor for Oxygen's Web site oomph.net. Her long-term compelling vision is to establish the Reach Back Foundation. This foundation will enable successful African American consultants to mentor and coach other women from the African diaspora in the areas of business development and entrepreneurship, using Warm Spirit as the paradigm for wealth creation and empowerment.

Nadine is also a wife and the mother of two children, Camilla and Isaiah. She lives in Exeter, New Hampshire, at Phillips Exeter Academy with her husband, Rev. Robert H. Thompson.

**Angela E. Soper** is a freelance writer, media consultant, and documentary filmmaker based in Salt Lake City, Utah. For nine years (1996-2005) she worked as the creative director/screenwriter  in the Visual Productions Department of Nu Skin Enterprises, a billion dollar, worldwide network-marketing company located in Provo, Utah. While she was at Nu Skin, Angela's work as a corporate video screenwriter won numerous awards in the industrial film category. She also cowrote the company's twentieth anniversary hardcover book, *Journey,* which was recognized in *Print* magazine's 2005 Regional Design Annual and in *Graphic Design USA* (June 2005). She has written for

Pax Television, the *Washington Post, People* magazine, and the *Salt Lake Tribune,* as well as for regional publications in Indiana, Virginia, and Utah.

Angela is currently coproducing/directing and writing the documentary *It Happened in Farmland,* a film about small towns and their struggles to survive, brought to light in one community's conflict between preserving the past and destroying it to make way for the modern. The documentary features an endangered historic courthouse and seven senior bridge-club women from a small Indiana town who posed for a controversial calendar to protest the building's slated destruction.

As a writer and a television and radio personality, Angela has interviewed or written material for numerous celebrities, including actors Hal Holbrook, Sir Anthony Hopkins, and Brad Pitt, as well as television host and producer Dick Clark and former Chrysler chairman Lee Iacocca.

# Other Titles in the Social Venture Network Series

## Values-Driven Business

*How to Change the World, Make Money, and Have Fun*
**Ben Cohen and Mal Warwick**

Written by high-profile entrepreneurs Ben Cohen (cofounder of Ben & Jerry's) and Mal Warwick, this engaging, accessible guide points the way to a new, socially responsible business ethic and offers entrepreneurs and owners the practical how-to tools they need to embed their values in their businesses.

## True to Yourself

*Leading a Values-Based Business*
**Mark Albion**

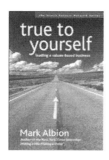

From the author of *New York Times* best-seller *Making a Life, Making a Living*® comes the ultimate leadership guide for socially responsible small businesses and entrepreneurs.

# Marketing That Matters

*10 Practices to Profit Your Business and Change the World*
**Chip Conley and Eric Friedenwald-Fishman**

Award-winning marketers Chip Conley and Eric Friedenwald-Fishman prove that "marketing" is not a dirty word—instead, it's key to advancing both the value and values of any business. They offer a thorough and practical guide to selling what you do without selling out who you are.

# Growing Local Value

*How to Build Business Partnerships That Strengthen
  Your Community*

**Laury Hammel and Gun Denhart**

Laury Hammel and Gun Denhart Hanna Andersson
founder Gun Denhart and BALLE co-founder Laury
Hammel show how every aspect of a business (from
product creation to employee recruitment to vendor
selection) holds the dual promise of bigger profits and
a stronger local community.

# About Berrett-Koehler Publishers

**Berrett-Koehler** is an independent publisher dedicated to an ambitious mission: Creating a World That Works for All.

We believe that to truly create a better world, action is needed at all levels—individual, organizational, and societal. At the individual level, our publications help people align their lives with their values and with their aspirations for a better world. At the organizational level, our publications promote progressive leadership and management practices, socially responsible approaches to business, and humane and effective organizations. At the societal level, our publications advance social and economic justice, shared prosperity, sustainability, and new solutions to national and global issues.

A major theme of our publications is "Opening Up New Space." They challenge conventional thinking, introduce new ideas, and foster positive change. Their common quest is changing the underlying beliefs, mind-sets, institutions, and structures that keep generating the same cycles of problems, no matter who our leaders are or what improvement programs we adopt.

We strive to practice what we preach—to operate our publishing company in line with the ideas in our books.

At the core of our approach is *stewardship,* which we define as a deep sense of responsibility to administer the company for the benefit of all of our "stakeholder" groups: authors, customers, employees, investors, service providers, and the communities and environment around us.

We are grateful to the thousands of readers, authors, and other friends of the company who consider themselves to be part of the "BK Community." We hope that you, too, will join us in our mission.

# Be Connected

## Visit Our Website

Go to www.bkconnection.com to read exclusive previews and excerpts of new books, find detailed information on all Berrett-Koehler titles and authors, browse subject-area libraries of books, and get special discounts.

## Subscribe to Our Free E-Newsletter

Be the first to hear about new publications, special discount offers, exclusive articles, news about bestsellers, and more! Get on the list for our free e-newsletter by going to www.bkconnection.com.

## Participate in the Discussion

To see what others are saying about our books and post your own thoughts, check out our blogs at www.bkblogs.com.

## Get Quantity Discounts

Berrett-Koehler books are available at quantity discounts for orders of ten or more copies. Please call us toll-free at (800)929-2929 or email us at bkp.orders@aidcvt.com.

## Host a Reading Group

For tips on how to form and carry on a book reading group in your workplace or community, see our website at www.bkconnection.com.

## Join the BK Community

Thousands of readers of our books have become part of the "BK Community" by participating in events featuring our authors, reviewing draft manuscripts of forthcoming books, spreading the word about their favorite books, and supporting our publishing program in other ways. If you would like to join the BK Community, please contact us at bkcommunity@bkpub.com.

# Books For ALL Kinds of Readers

At ReadHowYouWant we understand that one size does not fit all types of readers. Our innovative, patent pending technology allows us to design new formats to make reading easier and more enjoyable for you. This helps improve your speed of reading and your comprehension. Our EasyRead printed books have been optimized to improve word recognition, ease eye tracking by adjusting word and line spacing as well as minimizing hyphenation. Our EasyRead SuperLarge editions have been developed to make reading easier and more accessible for vision-impaired readers. We offer Braille and DAISY formats of our books and all popular E-Book formats.

We are continually introducing new formats based upon research and reader preferences. Visit our web-site to see all of our formats and learn how you can Personalize our books for yourself or as gifts. Sign up to Become A **RHYW** Registered Reader.

[www.readhowyouwant.com](www.readhowyouwant.com)

Made in the USA
Lexington, KY
10 September 2017